Professional Potpourri

Also by Dr. Margaret A. Golton
Unlock Your Potential: Know Your Brain and How It Works
Your Brain At Work: A New View of Personality and Behavior

Professional Potpourri:

Seeds Are Sown

Dr. Margaret A. Golton

FRANK PUBLICATIONS   New York

Library of Congress Cataloging in Publication Data

Golton, Margaret A.
   Professional Potpourri.

   1. Psychotherapy—Addresses, essays, lectures.
   2. Neuropsychology—Addresses, essays, lectures.
   3. Insurance, Health—United States—Addresses, essays,
   lectures. I. Title.
   RC480.G655   1984   150   84-13775

ISBN 0-942952-02-2

Published by
Frank Publications
60 East 42nd. St.
Suite 757
New York, NY 10017

To Gene
and
Our Many Children by Proxy

Contents

Preface

Professional Potpourri: Seeds Are Sown is a compilation of writings covering the 10-year period 1971–1980. The timing of its publication is reader inspired. My first book *Unlock Your Potential: Know Your Brain and How It Works*, based on recent brain research findings, was published in April 1982. It brought requests for other writings. In the meantime my second book, *Your Brain at Work: A New View of Personality and Behavior* was published in the fall of 1983. Since the second book proclaimed a major discovery of significance to educators, clinicians, parents and do-it-yourselfers, a retrospective of my intellectual excursions and my point of view seemed in order. Hence, *Professional Potpourri: Seeds are Sown.*

As I reviewed my many writings, I discovered in a paper written in 1971 the seeds of the discovery that surfaced in February 1983. Amazing but not unique. The brain is fertile terrain. What it does with seeds that are sown often remains privy to itself alone. One is not conscious of the process. One is not conscious of the interlockings, the fusions of ideas that occur. New insights come as a surprise. Discoveries are not anticipated. The brain has monitored, selected, stored, discarded according to its own guidelines. Conscious awareness that something of significance has occurred is accompanied by the impulse to shout: Eureka! Eureka! But there is not likely to be anyone to listen or hear or care. Discoveries are disconcerting. They rock the established. They dislocate the familiar. In a world such as ours where disarray abounds, discoveries are not likely to find a welcome mat irrespective of their pertinence or effectiveness, especially where personality and behavior are concerned. There is too little in this area that we know for sure. Hopes for a unified theory of personality have been dashed too many times, and parts continue to fall short of explaining the whole.

I have been fortunate. There has been in my professional world, I-CAPP (International Conference for the Advancement of Private Practice in Social Work), established in 1961. Its founders were the rebels, the mavericks, the dissenters in the social work profession. Had it been possible the profession would have disenfranchised them. It was not possible. These rebels, mavericks, dissenters were experienced, knowledgeable, skilled practitioners. They knew what they knew. They knew what they knew how to do. What they knew and what they knew how to do was not institution-bound. They were courageous. They were determined. There were among them many change agents, adventurers, charting new trails, taking trial runs into the emerging world.

I am grateful to I-CAPP; Grateful that it has been; grateful that it is. A rarity in its own right, it has provided a forum for the intellectual excursions my brain has chosen to undertake. It has no responsibility for the terrain my brain has explored. Certainly, it has no responsibility for the vistas I have discovered. I value the friendships that have bridged professional disparities. I value the incentive I-CAPP has provided to examine, to explore, to discover, to invent. My profound appreciation to its founders and the very special coterie of individuals who have carried on its task.

University Heights, Ohio   M.A.G.
May 1984

CHAPTER **1**

In Preparation for Immortality:*
How to Equip Children
to Live 150 Years
or More

*There comes a time when a traveler "must synchronize his
watch so it reads the time of the world he is heading for."*
Alfred Fabre-Luce

It is difficult to focus on the future when the world seems to be
a massive powder keg and there is doubt that it will survive the
day. One thing is clear: should the world come to an end and
all the people in it, so too will all of our worries. It is only in the
event of survival that we must muster our thoughts and energies
for action. It is to this eventuality, that the world will survive as
well as the majority of the people in it, that this exposition is
undertaken.

The issue of world survival is itself multidimensional: physical,
social, psychological. Ecology knows no national boundaries. Air
and water pollution on continents thousands of miles away may
eventually affect breathing capabilities of people in New York
and San Francisco and the digestive systems of persons eating

* Presented at the 10th Annual Meeting of CAPP (Conference for the Advancement of
Private Practice), Aspen, Colorado, June 16, 1971.

salmon and caviar. As is characteristic of the human condition, it has taken us many years to suddenly become aware of the long-range and side effects of industrialization. Scientists realize that what they need now is equipment that will monitor the air and waters over the earth and computers to anticipate the effect, short and long range, of the changes man is making in his environment. With nuclear energy, satellites, lasers and the ever-expanding science of genetics at his command, who would be willing to say that such instrumentation is not possible?

The greatest lag lies in the field of human relations. We have not yet had a Copernicus, a Newton or an Einstein to establish the basic laws of human reaction and interaction. There are at least 27 personality theories, each with its own methods and procedures for inducing change: adaptive, corrective, rehabilitative. Comparative analyses of these theories for a possible common core have been sketchy and have not yielded conclusions that are generally accepted and applied. Instead both theories and methods are proliferating. It is doubtful that world leaders looking for guides and methods to achieve international relationships consistent with the new world conditions created by our advanced technology will find the ruminations of psychology, psychiatry and social work helpful.

Be that as it may, there remains within the immediate bailiwick of personality experts some truly pressing problems. It is to these I wish to address myself. But first let me structure the world that is upon us as I see it; for it is only against this backdrop that the urgency of the issues I am presenting will become clear.

Current Realities

Few would disagree that the world and its inhabitants have been torn from the traditional moorings. Copernicus' view that the world as we know it is not one alone but one of countless in the universe has been incontrovertibly established. Convictions are mounting that species much on the order of man may inhabit other planets. Among the "flying saucer" enthusiasts one finds even stronger conviction that interplanetary communication is already a reality.

Intercontinental travel and communications satellites have made the "one world" fantasy a reality. The many continents that make up the earth are linked by sight, sound and physical contact. It is being projected that international industry will effect international cooperation and international control of power—something that neither diplomacy nor military might have been able to achieve. Today more than at any other time in the known history of man the destiny of man is the destiny of all men. Military confrontation may be localized but the side effects are worldwide. Malnutrition may be limited but the diseases it may spawn may spread quickly over large areas of the world. Such being the reality, we may anticipate that wars will stop not because there are no longer aggressive, power-hungry men or nations but because the side effects of war are too hazardous. The peoples of the world will be fed not out of any humanitarian impulse but out of a concern for human survival.

From universe to world to community—the immediate world in which each of us live: here, too, the old moorings are gone. Marriage is no longer a foregone conclusion; neither are children as an integral part of marriage. Young adults are experimenting with group relationships, polygamy, polyandry, homosexuality as well as the single life. Young unmarried women are preferring to keep their babies and parents are making this possible. Single women and men are being permitted by social agencies to adopt children. In more and more divorces, it is agreed that the children will remain with their fathers. The efficacy of the nuclear family is being seriously challenged. From it has emerged the drug culture of adults and children, massive biological and psychological breakdown among children and adults, frustration, apathy. Perhaps it is not the nuclear characteristic that is at fault, at least not in isolation. Perhaps contributing to the ill effects has been spatial mobility, industrial exploitation of human energy, an overly structured, stylized educational system.

One thing has become abundantly clear these last few years. Affluence does not give meaning to living. Perhaps here we can learn from the space program. It was not until Apollo 14 that the astronauts aimed to carry out systematic scientific projects. Up to that time efforts had been directed to the development of instruments and skills. Perhaps nineteenth- and twentieth-century man has been similarly engaged—in the development of instruments and skills necessary for the full experiencing of life. This then becomes the challenge of the present, and the unending challenge of the future: how to *enjoy* life to its fullest.

Instrumentation

Let us look first at the instruments available to us for pursuing this experience we call "life."

It is difficult to believe that air travel had its beginnings as recently as 1923. Then the longest passenger flight was 90 miles. During the period 1927–1939, air travel was opened to the Caribbean, South America, the Pacific, the Atlantic. In 1942, air travel encompassed the world. Today there is talk that within a few years one will be able to rocket from New York to London in 20 minutes. One can already breakfast in London and be back in New York for dinner.

But speedier than air travel will be transcontinental television-telephones. One will be able to hold worldwide conferences via television-telephone without leaving one's desk whether that desk is in one's office or in one's home. It is difficult to project the ramifications of this development. Perhaps father-absenteeism will no longer undermine the strength of the nuclear family.

There is the possibility also that the home will become again the cultural center for the family. This time with electronic technology bringing into the home via TV and radio cassettes the best of art, music, science, literature and, via an instant news relay system, history-in-the-making. Since the development of the long-playing record in 1940, free choice of auditory experience has been available on a massive scale. With the development of TV cassettes the same will be true for visual experience.

There are communities in which milk trucks are delivering and picking up radio cassettes much as rural libraries have done with books for years. It is estimated that cartrivision sets will be available for home use by spring 1971 at a cost of $900. By 1980, 30 million cassette movies should be on the market. The movie *I Am Curious (Yellow)* is already available for $60. One cassette cartridge of 80,000 visuals weighs less than one pound and if mass produced, say 2000 of one issue, can cost as little as $18.50 each. One publisher is already collaborating with a university professor to put a complete course in elementary chemistry on TV cartridges. Such a course would require approximately 20 cassettes and reading material.

R. Scott Hersey, the 29-year-old president of Hersey Video Systems, estimates that an individual of average ability would be able to earn a bachelor's degree in 180 hours of video cassette training. Courses are being offered now in aviation, securities, real estate, languages and self-motivation. Mr. Hersey estimates that stockbrockers can be trained in a matter of weeks instead of the usual three months required for traditional methods and procedures. He estimates that the average nine-year-old can learn in two days of video cassette training, which includes a textbook, all that he needs to know to pass aviation ground tests. He projects that policemen and salesmen can be trained more quickly and efficiently via TV cassettes than is possible by the usual methods.

Others are projecting that with the coaxial cable—the equivalent of a 60-lane highway as compared with a country road, or Nigara Falls as compared with a garden hose—home reception will be unlimited. With the flick of a switch one will be able to receive a facsimile of a newspaper, conduct library research on any subject, read the gas meter and watch for intruders.[1]

One will be able to make one's own cassettes. One will be able to record in one's home during one's absence programs on the public TV system.

By the end of 1970, 25 countries were already tied in to the Intersat system of communications. Another 10 are expected to join in 1971 and an additional seven in 1972. The cost of this has been reduced from $25,000 per year to $1000. Three satellites beams will cover most of the earth's surface. These satellites, 56 inches in diameter, 41 inches in length and weighing 334 pounds, will be stationed 25,000 miles over the equator and will be repairable on the spot. By 1985, broadcasts via satellite directly to home, office, school are foreseeable.

With international communication, individual and mass available, with international tourism the largest single industry and international economic enterprise already in development, it is difficult to imagine that a pluralistic federal world government can be far behind.[2] Perhaps it will be the economic sector of society that will achieve this as it has achieved many other things far beyond the imagination of the average man. Perhaps what we will need in addition to our technical instruments will be an "international league of minds," a world community of students and scholars to envisage, structure and implement a central world body which, like the conductor of an orchestra, will keep each part of the world functioning at its maximum and in the best interest of all. Monumental as this proposal may be, we must remember that it is easier to make big changes than small ones.[3]

Projections

Coupled with the electronic realities are genetic and sociological projections. Geneticists are predicting that by the year 2091, or 120 years from now, immortality will be among the choices available to man. An injection at birth will set up a cell regeneration process so that at the point of maximum cell maturity, 25 years, the cell is replaced. The body, the mind and all of the vital processes will not age beyond the point of maximum cell maturity. In fact, just a few weeks ago it was announced on radio that within 10 years it will be possible for medical science to stop the aging process *and* reverse it. To what point reversal will be possible and for how long was not specified.

To those who despair at this prospect Pablo Casals at 93 has a word of reassurance: ". . . age is a relative matter. If you continue to work and absorb the beauty in the world about you, you find that age does not necessarily mean getting old, at least not in the ordinary sense." Of himself he says: "I feel many things more intensely than ever before and life grows more fascinating."

There are in the United States, today, over seven million individuals who have passed age 75, and 10,000 who have passed the century mark. In the Ural Mountains of the USSR 84 persons out of 100,000 live to be over 100. Research teams for years now have been studying life in that area for clues to longevity.

Along with projections dealing with the aging process and longevity, are those dealing with propagation. It is predicted that before long, an injection at birth will inhibit the usual fertility cycle. This cycle will be activated chemically at the point where a man and woman decide that they wish to have children. Many other projections are afoot in the area of procreation: the control of sex and genetic inheritance; the fertilized ovum being carried to term in the womb of a woman who is not the biological parent; the creation of life *in vitro*. As has been true of each of man's major achievements, the potentials and the hazards are beyond man's fullest comprehension with the mental equipment currently at his disposal. If ever the eight billion brain cells estimated to be dormant are activated perhaps we will be better equipped to address ourselves to the possible eventualities.

Another projection pertinent to this exposition is that of sociologists. Paul Goodman estimates that an individual may be required to work one year in seven or a total of six or seven years to earn what is necessary for his basic maintenance. This work would be related to what society needs and not to what his special skills and interests might be. If the individual wanted a standard of living higher than the minimum he might then engage in occupations of his preference. The five-day forty-hour week has been a reality for some time. Some occupations now are striving for the long weekend with the work week only four days. In some occupations, senior employees are entitled to 13 weeks vacation a year. Free time is going to be in abundance with competition rampant among leisure-time activities.

The combination of long life (without the debility of aging) and extensive leisure (with affluence) poses problems the forerunners of which we are already experiencing. There is the expansion of drug use into all levels of society, the instability of the institution of marriage, the upheaval in education, the restlessness of youth, the panic of adults, the despair and dislocation of our elders. Each new advance in human experience always has brought dislocation, discontent, worry and despair. But there is something about the pervasiveness of the current situation—automation, electronic computers and communication, rocketry, miniaturization—that defies imagination and eludes comprehension.

Space exploration requires a new concept of the universe and the earth's place in it. Reproductive processes within the control of man (the initiation of life and the systematic determination of genetic characteristics), prevention, possibly reversal of the aging process will require of man that he bring under scrutiny all tradition, and taboos, biases and values. There is a starkness to the age-old philosophical question: what is it all about, somehow more gross against a backdrop of affluence and multiple choice than when people had to worry about sustenance, the basics of living.

I remember vividly my reactions at the International Conference of Social Work in 1967. I was almost envious of the underdeveloped countries. All they had to be concerned about was how to feed, clothe, house and educate their people. How elementary and simple this was compared to the task that faced us: to help people find value, purpose, challenge, self-fulfillment with minimum time and energy devoted to the basics of living. What would be the source of self-worth with money and possessions and job status no longer at a premium? There is no sadder man than the millionaire who works 14 hours a day to amass more millions but finds in all of this no sense of achievement or fulfillment, yet he doesn't know what else to do. His is a kind of personal poverty that could become the prototype of the future unless we take a long, fresh look at the world that is emerging, and what that world will offer and require of those who are alive in it.

Change: How to Effect It

Resistance to this task is all about us: What about the atomic bomb, water and air pollution, and the myriad other forces of potential destruction? It is almost as though there is comfort in the prospect of doom. There are amazingly few people who look upon the potential of longevity and ultimately immortality with any sense of excitement or challenge. The most common reaction is: "Who needs it?" What an indictment of our society and culture! What a handicap in preparing the younger generations for what lies ahead.

We may take heart from one of Margaret Mead's observations. In her follow-up study of the people of Manus, she observed that it takes a "coherent adult culture in miniature . . . to bring up children in a new tradition." That is, adults must change first. But the change does not have to occur in a large number of adults, or through large-scale education. A small group of gifted, imaginative individuals can develop and establish the necessary patterns.

Another of her observations may have pertinence for us. Total change—new patterns without reminders of the old (traditions, taboos)—is more effective than modifications of the old. Is it possible that our young adults who join communes as well as those who are venturing relationships outside the traditional structure of marriage and family are doing just this: making a complete break from the old in order to establish the new which hopefully will be better suited to the world that is emerging? There is another parallel. When Dr. Mead began her study on Manus in 1928, she found the youth restless and disenchanted. Delinquency, sexual escapades and runaways were rampant. The youth were not only indifferent to the adult world but actively subordinating and destructive.[4]

In other words, what we are probably experiencing in this last third of the twentieth century are the rumblings, the dislocations, the disenchantment and despair that presage and accompany extensive social change. Important beyond measure is how the existing societal structures and current leadership will respond. Upon this response very likely will rest the manner in which the necessary changes are effected: whether by impulsive destruction or planful, imaginative innovation. One thing is true, the young adults of today are better educated, better informed, more traveled than any other generation in recorded history. They have known security and plenty and a world marred by relatively minor, highly localized military destruction for almost 20 years. The song: "Is That All There Is?" might well be their theme song with "All I Want Is Everything" their motto. And who is to say what the limits of "everything" may be? There are some theorists who venture that even war may turn out to be a transitory form of behavior in human cultural history, a time-limited stage in human progress. In its present depersonalized form war no longer meets the need for brotherhood as it has in the past. Man may be able to find in sports, in travel, in adventure, nondestructive outlets for his aggressive energies. And it is very possible that with his potential for innovation he will be able to invent peace just as he has invented war.

Social Changes: Incipient

The readiness with which we tend to despair when alerted to the negative side effects of our achievements (pollution, etc.) betrays what seems to me a basic lack of confidence in the human species, comfort in the sense of doom or a pervasive fear of man's ultimate potential. Perhaps we do need to have conservationists to spot the devastating effects of the denuding of the forests by industry. Perhaps we do need to have Nader's Raiders to expose exploitation and carelessness. Perhaps there was a time when indifference, exploitation, abuse were considered the prerogative of the industrial system.

There are indications today that this is no longer so. U.S. Steel announces that it is engaging not only in reforestation, but is developing wildlife preserves and areas of natural beauty. Industries are beginning to recycle waste products (abandoned automobiles, cans, newspapers) so that less strain will be placed on natural resources. Scientists have developed a plastic that destroys itself. In 1967, Ford rejected an American-designed pollution-free auto. It is now in production in Japan and should be on the market in 1972.

Emerging also are signs of social consciousness on the part of big business. In some communities banks are establishing daycare centers and on a high level of professional service. Currently, a pharmaceutical concern is establishing throughout the country a high-level homemaking service ranging from the simplest of home maintenance skills to professional care of the aged, children, the acutely and chronically ill.

One begins to find in the literature reference to humanizing industry, i.e., structuring tasks to take into account the social and psychological needs of people as well as families. One is finding, also, beginning concern for beautifying cities and planning communities with people rather than industry as the focus. There are already "vest pocket" parks in Washington, D.C., including play areas for children and sitting areas for the elderly. Plans for a similar area in Cleveland were announced just a few days ago. Tokyo closed off its downtown area and set up sidewalk cafes. Not only was pollution reduced but retail sales went up 50 percent.

What seems most difficult for us at this point in time is to realize that each new developing in knowledge, in skill exerts broad influence on development strategy in a technologically advanced society. It does not occur to us that if we exhaust certain natural resources we will either find ways to replenish them or we will find substitutes. (Nuclear energy has virtually replaced coal). In other words where natural science is concerned we must not underestimate the imagination, the resourcefulness, the inventiveness of man. Hopefully the same potentials exist in the biological and psychological sciences. We need only to devote as much time, attention and money to their development. Richard Meier suggests that the retraining of people for the world of the future can be viewed as a salvaging operation much as industry views the recycling of its worn or outdated products.[5]

Goals

Probably for the first time in the history of man we are experiencing a reverse transmission of culture. Children know more than their parents. The young are experiencing the world in a way that it has never been experienced before. Kahil Gibran anticipated this in 1923 when he wrote in *The Prophet*, "On Children."

> Your children are not your children.
> They are the sons and daughters of Life's longing for itself.
> They come through you but not from you,
> And though they are with you yet they belong not to you.
>
> You may give them your love but not your thoughts,
> For they have their own thoughts.

You may house their bodies but not their souls,
For their souls dwell in the house of tomorrow,
    which you cannot visit, not even in your dreams.
You may strive to be like them, but seek not to make
    them like you.
For life goes not backward nor tarries with yesterday.

Margaret Mead suggests that for those over 30, contemplating the world today is like learning a new culture. Not only are the problems in society and the world new, but there is such discontent with the old goals and values. There is disillusionment with a society that values things above people, that exploits the environment instead of developing it for the enrichment of living.

The new frontier that is coming into view is the human potential. Needed to pursue this are opportunities for developing the aesthetic, romantic, affective faculties of man as well as the intellectual. Needed also is a perception of man as a growing organism with ability to adapt and invent, and who needs to appreciate the fact that he can make his own future happen. The challenge of competition needs to give way to the enrichment of cooperation; the comfort in sameness needs to give way to the excitement of difference and the unknown. Alexander Pushkin poses that "higher human needs are insatiable. Information," he says, "can enrich man's positive emotions and positive emotions play a great part in the higher mental activity of man." [6]

It is estimated that today men know a hundred times more than they did in 1900. And in the field of physics alone, knowledge is said to double every four years. With this as a frame of reference it is understandable that some educators pose that no degree be considered valid after ten years. One sees here and elsewhere beginning evidence of a changing perception of education from a time-limited to a lifelong enterprise, though not necessarily under the auspices of an educational institution. One is beginning to find evidence, also, that talented aptitude as well as education in the "school of life" are being rediscovered and freshly assessed. Schooling has been a major screening device for many years. The assumption has been that increased schooling improved job performance. Research findings in textile industries, utility installations and department stores (nonmanagerial) have proven these assumptions to be invalid.[7,8]

In a technologically advanced society and in a community that literally encompasses the world, there is little doubt that education is important. But perhaps the age-old questions need to be engaged again, education to what end? Why was it assumed that education would increase productivity or effectiveness in a work situation? Is that what it was intended to do? If it is not to increase productivity or effectiveness, what is the aim of education? What should it be? These questions take on added cogency in the light of automation and longevity.

In addressing itself to these questions, society must take its eyes off the path it has travelled and focus on the new horizons that are coming into view. What kind of life experiences, what kind of academic underpinning, what kind of intellectual skills does an individual need to equip him for living in a world where change is the only certainty; where deviation and difference are commonplace; where choices are multiple, each of course with its price; where in the midst of crowds he will often be alone; where kinship ties may offer rootedness only in fantasy.

The world toward which society must focus its attention is fraught with dangers. With possibilities unlimited, one may decide that nothing is important. Without the "must" there may be no "will." Without the psychological equipment to use leisure meaningfully, there may be the degeneracy of apathy, despair, impotence.

The openness required by a world of variety and change is difficult to achieve and maintain. The autonomy necessary for self-direction and self-motivation must be rooted in a firm sense of self—one's uniqueness, aptitudes, interests, frailties. An open-ended lifespan poses a challenge to purpose, to values, indeed to a philosophy of living. The question "Why am I here?" has been asked throughout the ages. Today as perhaps never before the question remains for each individual to answer for himself. He is the one who must chart the course and make the choices that occur along the way. Life has "happened" to him. He will decide what to make of that "happening."

Basic Equipment

What equipment does the individual bring to the life experience? "No one ever recovers from the fact that he was born an individual," says Roger J. Williams.[9] We have been through a period of giving lip service to the uniqueness of each individual. Our major efforts have been directed to categorizing and ultimately homogenizing the species. The categorization efforts can be seen as part of instrumentation to be placed hopefully, in the service of individuals. The homogenization efforts, I think, will eventually fall into the classification of trial and error, a developmental necessity spawned by rapid social change, mounting population and burgeoning knowledge without adequate instruments or human skill.

What we must once again address ourselves to is that each individual has his own unique structure of brain cells, emotions, bone and muscular structure and glandular patterns. Each has his own distinctive pattern of eating, sleeping, crying, loving, learning, moving. Since each human infant comes into a social situation, his distinctive patterns are immediately subjected to modification. It is not likely that this will change. Socialization is a necessity. What must emerge as we face the future is greater clarity as to which distinctive characteristics must be modified so that the individual may live in a heavily populated society, and which must be preserved and cultivated so that he may have a full and meaningful life experience. In other words, even in child rearing we must differentiate between instrumentalities and goals. We must affirm, perhaps with greater commitment than ever before, that each man has his own way to achieve life, liberty, and the pursuit of happiness, and the right to it.

There are some people for whom it is enough to have food, shelter, clothing. Others strive for self-fulfillment. In between there are many variations. Similarly, there are individuals who want only to know how to do certain tasks. They do not want to know why one does it that way. Nor are they concerned with finding or developing better ways. What makes for these differences is not yet known. With modern technological equipment and automation it may be possible to pull together the mental, physical, chemical characteristics of the technician, the theorist, the inventor, the educator, the therapist, and examine the relationships and life experiences of each. Such analysis might lead to knowledge on the heredity-environment conundrum, and provide guides to future education.

In the meantime, as we consider the new world that looms before us, spatially, technologically, interrelationally, we must take a truly pristine look at the human being, his basic equipment and his potentials. One writer suggested that each newborn infant should be viewed as a new species. This draws even more starkly the nurturing task than did Margaret Mead's observation some years ago that two children born 10 years apart in the same family live in two different worlds.

Among the intrinsic capabilities of the human species are the five senses: sight, hearing, taste, smell, touch; the mental processes of thought, memory, perception, anticipation, imagination; the affective mechanisms for experiencing and expressing love, hate, anger, approval, disapproval; the motor equipment to sit, stand, walk, run, jump, dance, swim, play ball, sew, knit, weave, crochet, paint, sculpt, build, tear down, singly or in multiple combination. Given man's manifold capabilities in a society of rapidly unfolding possibilities one is faced with an incomprehensively complex task.

The Task

Adults as they aim to equip children for living face a threefold task: 1. *socialization*, helping the child develop the skills necessary for living with people; 2. *individuation*, helping him develop a firm sense of self; and 3. *actuation*, helping him develop the psychological, social, academic, technical skills he needs for self-expression and self-realization.

Socialization

To be an acceptable member of a crowded, technological society, the individual must be able to manage with a minimum of energy and discomfort and maximum of flexibility his basic physical needs—eating, sleeping, eliminating. He must be aware of and accepting of different lifestyles and values where basic physical needs are concerned. He must learn early that his freedom ends with the other fellow's nose; and eventually, that courtesy and consideration beget courtesy and consideration just as antagonism begets antagonism. As a member of a world community with mankind his neighbor, he needs to look upon difference with interest, curiosity and as a potential source of enrichment. Together with the feeling of belonging from which he derives comfort and security he needs interest—and determination in "becoming." The unfamiliar and the untried should pose challenge, and stimulate investigation and inventiveness. Clannishness and status rooted in homogeneity are atavistic. They have no place in a community that encompasses the world.

Individuation

Mechanization and a highly stylized way of life are incompatible with individuation. Little wonder that for the past several generations we have been so preoccupied with norms and patterns of behavior and control. The newborn member of the human species had to be acclimated as quickly as possible to the routines and the procedures of the particular family into which he had been born. It was his hard luck if his placid temperament did not match the high-speed tempo of his mother and the restless impatience of his father. No one took the time or the trouble to learn that his pattern of reaction was to light, sound, heat, cold, touch, adults, children. No one took the trouble to observe whether he accepted change easily or with distress. No one bothered to notice whether he preferred quiet or activity. The world was as it was and he was expected to adapt to it. What is more, he was expected to adapt in the same way as did those who had preceded him.

The life of the urban and suburban housewife is no haven of relaxation. Her chauffeuring schedule is often more demanding than the work schedule of her commuting husband. The number and variety of tasks for which she is responsible requires a high level of organization and efficiency. Little wonder that she has neither the time, inclination or interest in discovering what particular style of functioning her newborn brings to the world. It takes time, patience and interest to learn if an infant learns best via direction (schedule) or trial and error (self-demand); by being told or by watching. According to the psychologist, Dr. Benjamin Bloom, each child writes his own intellectual history by what he responds to in his environment. What tremendous, unrealistic pressure parents have put upon themselves when they have looked upon learning or developmental variance in their children as evidence of their failure. They have paid much too little attention, and given much too little credence, to the innate characteristics the individual child brought into the world with him. Along with recognition and acceptance of these characteristics must go faith that they will serve the individual well as he carves out his own particular niche in life, as he charts the particular road he will travel.

Parents are quick to protest that teachers do not individualize children. The protest under the present educational system in most cases is valid. But ask these same parents to give you a word profile of each of his children and they are numb. The present generation of parents has been too busy managing the mechanics of living, doing the multitudinous tasks that go along with their many roles to develop the skills required for the process of individuation where their children are concerned. Essential to individuation are sensitivity, perceptiveness, inquisitiveness, and above all else is excitement in the challenge of watching and influencing the development of a unique being, who is experiencing life for the first time, in his own particular way; a being who will himself leave an indelible mark that will be experienced by those who come after him. To develop the skills necessary for individuating, one must have time for hearing and listening, time for viewing and seeing, time for experiencing and feeling. With the advent of the automobile, radio, television, time for such matters has virtually disappeared. Perhaps this is one of the reasons that the young adults of today, suddenly acutely aware of the phenomenon of self, are seeing the lives of their parents as barren and things as sterile. Perhaps this is why one hears them so often speak in terms of returning to the farm, the simple life where there is time to just be.

Actuation

The family into which the child is born serves as the first mirror in which he sees himself. It is in his first years that he learns whether he is pretty or plain, bright or stupid, desired or tolerated. It is in his first years that he learns whether his worth and desirability are determined by who he is or by what he does, or perhaps by the aftermath of his acts. So often what he does brings results different from what he intended. (He was practicing ball-throwing and a window broke.)

Sometimes what he learns about himself in his family proves to be a fallacy. His parents may have made him feel that he was very bright. Yet when he went into the first grade he didn't know how to read; others learned faster than he did. His parents may have praised his art and put it on display. Yet his teacher barely noticed what he made.

What is more, the mirror provided by the family is multidimensional and multifaceted. It reflects thoughts, through speech, manner, actions. It reflects feelings, spoken, unspoken; intended, unconscious. Little wonder that a shy, sensitive 8-year-old develops a stutter. His mother, while still harboring an unconscious fear of the aggressiveness of men, is encouraging him to meet the physical assaults of his playmates with physical force. Little wonder that the son of a multitalented but unfulfilled father seeks only the simple tasks, those he can fulfill in one sitting. The complex, challenging enterprise draws his father like a magnet and he must step aside. A mother protests giving her 16-year-old daughter a clothing allowance. What if she demonstrates that she can manage money responsibly as she has all other tasks? The mother is then truly out of a job.

It is in the family that the individual has his first exposure to what is cherished and valued, what is resented and rejected, what one wishes for and what one dreads. Much of this reaches the child in subtle imperceptible ways. It is in the climate of the home. By osmosis rather than by precept does it penetrate and become an influence upon the child's perceptions and reactions. This is how a child learns whether life is an experience to be treasured or deplored as a burden; whether growing is a challenge or an inevitability to be borne; whether mastery is an achievement or an obligation; whether learning is exciting or a chore. This is where he learns if there is only one right way or whether there is respect for and intrigue in difference.

What we must eventually reckon with is that actuation is not the same for all. To some self-realization will come from tradition, from interest in and love of the past. For some, in order to develop their potentials, there will need to be the structured setting, the prescribed course of study and an established sequence as well as the active guidance and encouragement of the educator. These resources should and must be available. At the same time, for those individuals who require more freedom in what, how, when and in what setting they learn the flexibility that our burgeoning technocracy makes possible must be brought into play.

Socialization is a tooling-up process. It provides the child with the patterns of behavior that will serve him efficiently and with a minimum of conscious effort to function in society. Individuation should provide the child with a sense of self: what makes him, him; where he ends and someone else begins. It should provide him with a sense of his own rights, and the rights of others. He may have freedom, but his freedom ends with the other person's nose. He may have choice; but choice must be viewed within the context of responsibility. Actuation is the how-to-do-it of individuation: how do you become the individual you can and want to be, in the world in which you find yourself. It is with actuation that this paper really concerns itself. How can we fulfill our innate potential in a world-wide community, the boundaries of which are within easy reach, and where choices ultimately may be infinite. From the how-to-do-it will flow naturally the how-to-equip our children.

How-to-do-it

Where there is multiple-choice, one needs most of all to know what one wants. Where there is longevity, one can indulge one's self in wanting many things. Then there is only the question of which does one want to do first. It is estimated that today only one man in 1000 is engaged in work that utilizes his aptitudes, energies, initiative, and satisfies his interests. Long ago that was recognized as one of the hazards of the Industrial Revolution: that the interests of man would be sacrificed to the needs of the machine. We have come full circle: machine now can be put in the service of man; and man, once again can, in fact must, become the central focus in the world—not money, not technology, not space, but man and the fulfillment of his highest potential, his joy in living.

It has been estimated by Herbert Otto, Carl Rogers and the late Abraham Maslow that the healthy individual functions at perhaps 5 percent of his potential. Such estimates together with those that suggest that we are using only one half of our brain cells present possiblities that are truly beyond comprehension with our current equipment. Where human nature has been most seriously sold short, according to Maslow, has been in the development of his capacity for happiness, joy, kindness, generosity, peace of mind, fun, the sense of well-being.[10]

In the light of these projections, it would seem that the most indispensable characteristic in the human personality would be *open-endedness*: open-endedness in his perception of himself, in his perception of the life experience, in his perception of learning. There needs to be openness, too, to differences in people (racial, cultural, psychological). There needs to be acknowledgment and respect for differences in perceptions and values, though not necessarily acceptance. One would not aim for the sievelike personality, touched by everything but affected by nothing. One would aim instead for the type of personality that is interested in, and perhaps challenged by, difference and able to be selectively influenced by it. Not the chameleon but the kaleidoscope might be the symbol of future man—not fickleness but infinite variability as new bits and pieces of knowledge and experience are added to the equipment for living.

For open-endedness to be realized there needs to be an inner-rootedness. The anomie which has become a common phenomenon in our highly mobile society must be replaced by *autonomy*, coupled with autoplasticity (adaptability) and autostability (possessing an internal stabilizing mechanism). Most apt is the story of the Indian who, realizing he didn't know the way out of the woods affirmed: "Me not lost, wigwam lost." It is this me-ness that needs to be firmly entrenched in the human personality as pervasive and indestructible, whatever the circumstances the individual may find himself in. It is this me-ness that must be identified, nurtured, developed in children as they grow and prepare themselves for future-oriented living in a world community.

The sense-of-self will give guidance to "wants." Wants will provide guidelines to choice. With time no longer the automatic controller, an individual will be able to achieve many of his desires and exercise many choices. He will no longer have to make a lifetime commitment to a specific career at age 20 or 21. He will be able to change areas of interest and activity at any age, 50, 70, even 100, not necessarily because of frustration or dissatisfaction but because he is seeking new experiences, new challenges. Only recently a newspaper carried a feature story of a man who left business to become a psychologist, a woman who, after many years as a student counselor, became a professionally trained librarian, a banker who had become a biologist.

CLIMATE
Self-hood characterized by open-endedness and autonomy requires confidence and courage. "Healthy children," says Erikson, "will not fear life if their parents have integrity enough not to fear death." This is a tremendous challenge to parents. For while preparing their children for life-without-end they at the same time face the unrelenting fact that every moment of living is fraught with infinite dangers. One cannot for a moment forget that the human being at one and the same time is a creature of unfathomable potential and so fragile that too much water or a breath of air with the wrong ingredients can still him forever. With every advance in technology the risks and dangers are compounded. The task for every human being then becomes that of commitment to perenially new beginnings in the face of imminent, unpredictable, irreversible ending.

In this incontrovertible reality, lies the wisdom of planning life as though it goes on forever, but living each day as though it were the last. Pertinent to it, too, is the philosophy of the moment promulgated by a German philosopher long ago. All that is really ours is the "now." There is memory, of course, to keep the now in context. There is tomorrow which we can anticipate. But the now "is." It is to the using and appreciating the now, the moment of current experience, that we must learn to give attention, whether that current experience is doing, seeing, feeling, thinking, or just being.

Essentially the climate that is most propitious to the future-oriented child is the one that conveys the spirit: "Let's unpack and live" rather than "Let's wait until tomorrow," so rampant in our society. There are all too many people so engrossed in what they hope will be that they neither experience nor appreciate what is. Inevitably it all falls short and one ends up with "Is that all there is?" To approach each day as the miracle that it is, to approach each experience with expectation and readiness for challenge, these are gifts all too rarely given children by today's parents. One cannot give what one has not had. And too few of today's parents have had these gifts bequeathed to them. The tooling up for the automated society has been too demanding. It has diverted people from the intrinsics of life and living. That a relearning process is under way in our society is beginning to be evident in the movement toward individualizing education, allotting more funds for the arts, beautifying cities, thinking of industrial expansion not in terms of the maximum output but in terms of what is optimum for the benefit of man. These are considerations that had been lost sight of for many years except in the protestations of the philosophers and theorists.

STRUCTURE

With the frenzy of going, doing, seeing, hearing that characterizes our current society, children are in great danger of being time-poor. *Free time*—time to think, to feel, to do nothing, to just "be"—has become a truly rare commodity. It is a commodity, furthermore, which is certainly not sought or cherished. Curious this is, indeed, when one stops to realize that time is perhaps the most precious commodity of all. It is transitory. It is irreversible. It is irreplaceable. Why then do we squander it with such determination and equanimity? We create treadmills which we pursue assiduously. Social chitchat has become a fetish. Young people resort to drugs and communes to escape or avoid loneliness. The newly divorced catapult themselves into new marriages because they cannot tolerate solitude. Whatever sense of self we have seems to come from the outside and seems to need the confirmation of others.

To achieve a sense-of-self with internal roots, one must know who one is. One must know what one likes, what one dislikes; what one can do, what one cannot do; and how one affects others: is one liked or disliked, sought after, rejected. To achieve this knowing one must have *opportunities* to do: run, jump, skip, dance, play, work, draw, build, alone and with others. One must have *opportunities to experience and express reactions*: pleasure, displeasure, joy, pain, hurt, anger, loss, disappointment. The child's development as an independent, separate human being is furthered when he can (1) differentiate his words and thoughts from those of others; (2) when he realizes the difference between the spoken and the unspoken word, between thoughts that can be made public and those that must remain private; (3) when he, as audience to his own speech can monitor what he says so that he achieves the results he seeks. Just as the child must be helped to recognize the difference between the silent and the spoken word, so too he must be helped to realize the difference between the wish and the act: that wishing does not make it so; that wishes do not make things happen. Children learn early, if not consciously, that what they do makes a difference. If they cry they get attention. If they smile and coo, they receive smiles and cooing in return. If they defy, they incur disapproval, even anger. They test and retest the acts and responses so that both are predictable and ultimately within conscious control. The parent whose reactions are inconsistent or erratic leaves the child without this essential testing ground, without the opportunity to develop the skills with which to achieve the acceptance, the intimacy, the affirmation, the caring which is essential to human well-being.

Perhaps the most critical task of all in child rearing today, however, is the stimulating of curiosity, the development of imagination, the cultivating of a sense of wonder. There is no greater gift one can bequeath a child, says Rachel Carson, then an appreciation of the wonders that exist all about him—the marvel of a grain of sand, a snowflake, a rock, a stone; the magnificence of a thunder storm; the magnetism of the waves. Equipped with a sense of wonder, an individual no matter how many years he may live is never alone, can never fall victim to boredom or apathy. The intrigue of nature is literally boundless.[11] As for curiosity and imagination they are indispensable in a swift-changing world where it will be necessary to anticipate problems before they occur. Dealing only with the problems that already exist will be a luxury society will not be able to afford. The pragmatist dealing with historical facts in their interrelationships may become as extinct as the dodo bird who flew backwards, interested not in where he was going but only in where he had been. The world will belong to the futurist experienced in anticipatory imagination, who can project cause-and-effect relationships aided in a very practical sense by our highly advanced technology.

EXPERIENCE

From the moment of birth the individual requires a combination of solitude and society; privacy and companionship. His world is made up of people, things, events and time. There is the present, past, future, marked by the cyclical sequence of light and darkness, sleeping and being awake. He grows but he continues to be himself. His first attempts at mastery begin very early, perhaps with his first firm grip of his mother's finger or his first halting efforts to hold his bottle. His reaching-out efforts must be nurtured, encouraged. Opportunities for mastery should abound in his world, with the adults on the sidelines setting the expectations appropriate to his capacities, cheering his achievements, keeping him ever aware that there is a tomorrow in case his accomplishments fall short today. Adults need to build into the child's self-perception early that he is a learner and will always be. What he does not know or cannot do reflects not failure but rather his incompleteness. It should elicit not despair but challenge and the confidence that he can and will learn.

Parents must deny themselves the pleasure of doing for the youngster what he can do for himself. A child's request: "Draw me a picture" or "Build me a house" must be redirected and the child encouraged to accept the challenge of drawing and building himself for it is he who must learn what his own fingers and muscles are able to do. Similarly the child must be encouraged to work out his problems in his own way, perhaps with adult guidance but with his own thought process in full operation.

Clearly differentiated must be the tools (the child's basic equipment, physical, intellectual, emotional), the skills (what he is able to do and what he must still learn to do) and the task (the challenge, the chore, the responsibility). To rear autonomous, open-ended, inner-rooted people, respectful of their abilities and potentials, and motivated for achievement whether for economic gain or personal gratification, the environment must have fluidity. It must have the flexibility to adapt to the changes that come with maturation and with mastery. Respect for the impatience expressed when a challenge, having been mastered, becomes a chore promotes the move from learning to responsibility. Acknowledgment of the readiness for responsibility raises the issue of privileges. Children often and rightfully protest that they are given adult responsibilities but treated like children. Even more affronting and damaging is that parents so often do not really look upon their children as people. Much too often they see them as appendages to be pushed, pulled, dragged, or as puppets to be manipulated. Their disrespect is disguised in such colloquialisms as: "Is this O.K.?"; "We are going to do this. Is it all right?" "Do you want to go to bed now?" Actually the child has no choice but to follow the decisions and dictates of the parent however they may be couched.

Our society, too, presents irreconcilable dichotomies. At the same time that it demands of its populace mobility, autonomy, self-direction, the life experiences provided by the environment in which children grow provides ever fewer opportunities for children to go places on their own. Distances from place to place are so great transportation must be provided. Walking, riding bikes are activities fraught with danger rather than a source of satisfaction, freedom and self-development.

Changes in community planning are already under discussion. Changes in parenting behaviors are more difficult to effect because of the multiple pressures the current patterns of living place upon parents. Educating parents in the task of parenting might help, but parent educators would have to change their focus from concern with parental attitudes which is essentially a therapeutic task to equipping parents with knowledge about the developmental needs of their children and how best they can be met. On the part of experts this requires a change from the role of the enabler to that of the behavioral engineer, a readiness to make specific recommendations on specific behaviors to achieve specific goals. Perhaps the speediest way to achieve what needs to be done in child development is to train child-care experts to be available to families. Their primary task would be the development of children, each to his fullest individual potential. They would not be harassed by the many varied responsibilities that fall to the mother and housewife. Of course, there is the possibility that massive parent education via TV cassettes might prove as effective and fast as has been training for aviation and investments. It is indeed difficult to realize that the holdbacks of the past do not have to incapacitate the future.

The Challenge

Schools without walls, learning without failure, intimacy without marriage, parenthood without mating—these are phenomena already existent in our society. Perhaps for the first time in human history, there are within the confines of one culture a variety of lifestyles available with complete freedom of choice resting with the individual. Mobility, increasing leisure, knowledge and recreation literally at one's fingertips leave the individual truly the "captain of the ship and master of his soul." The risk of being without mooring, or guidelines or goals are great. For children and adults alike the watchword might well be: Be all you can, or better still, in the words of Goethe:

> Whatever you can do or dream you can, begin it.
> Boldness has genius, and power, and magic in it.

Notes

1. Friendly, Fred W., "Asleep at the Switch of the Wired City," *Saturday Review* (October 10, 1972), p. 58.

2. Michelson, Sig, "The First Eighty Years Toward the Global Village," *Saturday Review* (January 24, 1970), p. 22.

3. Editorial, "Toward a World University," *Saturday Review* (October 11, 1969).

4. Mead, Margaret, *New Lives for Old* (New York: Morrow, 1956), pp. 154, 366–446.

5. Meier, Richard, "The Metropolis and the Transformation of Resources," *Science and Public Affairs* (May 1970).

6. Pushkin, Alexander, "Genius and Villainy Are Two Things Incompatible," *Psychology Today* (August 1970), p. 54.

7. Kuhn, James W., "Would Horatio Alger Need a Degree?" *Saturday Review* (December 19, 1970), p. 54.

8. Berg, Ivor, "Education and Jobs: The Great Train Robbery," *Saturday Review* (December 19, 1970).

9. Williams, Roger J., "The Biology of Behavior," *Saturday Review* (January 30, 1970), p. 17.

10. Goble, Frank G., *The Third Force: The Psychology of Abraham Maslow*, in *Psychiatry and Social Science Review* (February 3, 1971), vol. 2.

11. Carson, Rachel, *The Sense of Wonder* (New York: Harper & Row, 1965).

CHAPTER 2

Maturational Therapy: A Specific Treatment Modality*

Treatment modalities have been proliferating at an unprecedented rate the past several years. Transactional Analysis, Gestalt, Encounter Groups, Primal Therapy, Behavioral Engineering have joined the ranks of the familiar Freudian, Rankian, Alderian, Jungian, Rogerian, Sullivanian et al. schools of psychic intervention. A messianic fervor seems to encompass the adherents of each as they develop their procedural patterns, their terminology, their philosophy. Much like the six blind men and the elephant, each presumes to have the one and only answer. What a gross distortion would have resulted had the view of the elephant been limited to that of the man who examined the tail, or the one who touched the leg or the side. A composite was necessary for the delineation of the whole.

It has been estimated that there are 27 personality theories, 52 procedural systems and 13 theories of personality change. Little wonder researchers only recently reported that they have isolated 70 different types of intelligence and estimate that there may be 50 more. Biologists estimate that only one half of the 15 billion cells in the human brain have been activated; and that the

* Presented at the 12th Annual Conference of the Conference for the Advancement of Private Practice in Social Work, Detroit, June 20–22, 1973.

most educated productive individuals use, at most 5 to 10 percent of these. The implications of these formulations are staggering. They preclude conclusions on the part of any individual as to exclusivity or singularity where the human personality is concerned.

To each instead falls [the] responsibility to search out, delineate, explicate (1) the specific dimension or dimensions of personality specific techniques tap and to what end; (2) why they work (for the technician it suffices to know that a procedure works; the professional practitioner must continue to search for the reason why); (3) the conditions necessary for effective, efficient, economical performance. There is a critical urgency to this task at this time in history.

Professionalism is under attack. Every profession is being subjected to scrutiny in terms of effectiveness, efficiency, economy. The tasks being undertaken by the professions are phenomenally complex. The instruments for determining effectiveness are almost less than primitive, but little credence is being given to this discrepancy. There is the danger that antiprofessionalism will lead to antiknowledge. In medicine the annual physical examination is suspect. People are being encouraged to let the body heal itself. In education, there are recurrent suggestions that formal schooling should be abandoned; that all of society should be the school, and every adult, a teacher. In mental health one finds increasing references to the importance of people reaching out to people. Every person can probably attest to the self-healing of the body and the mind; the effectiveness of the home remedy, of the intuitive human response—understanding, sympathy, empathy, patience. Every person has certainly experienced learning outside the classroom. But there are limits. There are limits to self-education. There are limits to self-healing, to the effectiveness of the home remedy, to the intuitive human response as a healing instrument. It is these limits that must be clarified. There is the danger that with all our knowledge and technical sophistication we may retreat to the primitive. There is danger that in our zeal to reestablish person-to-person communication we will underestimate the vulnerability of the psyche to hurt, to irreparable damage in the name of, in the guise of good intentions.

This presentation of Maturational Therapy has a twofold purpose. It is intended as a case in point, demonstrating the kind of delineation, explication, analysis, clinical social workers might well undertake as they face the open market in mental health, a population with many more options in practitioner choice than ever before, and a skeptical society demanding proof of effectiveness, efficency, economy. Secondly, it is an effort to establish the efficacy, the validity of personality change via the conscious, rational processes.

Theoretical and Perceptual Base

In the proliferation of treatment techniques a curious phenomenon has occurred. There are approaches to change via the unconscious, via the sensory system (touch), the affective system (emotive expression), via perception, via behavior. What has been noticeably lacking is an approach to change via conscious, rational processes. If one attempts to describe such a procedure one is likely to be summarily dismissed with, "Oh, that's intellectual." Yes, indeed. But who has yet established that change in perceptions, feelings, behavior is not possible through more accurate knowledge, more comprehensive understanding?

Maturational Therapy as herein promulgated is specific. It has form. It has content. It is rooted in a philosophy, a frame of reference. It is goal-directed. It is value-oriented. Its assumptions are explicit.

The practitioner is in the driver's seat. He presumes to know the psychosocial terrain of our society and culture. He presumes to know the human psyche, its strengths, its points of vulnerability. He knows where in the psychosocial experience to look for the roots of individual discomfort and malfunctioning, using as a frame of reference and a guide, knowledge that has accrued in the field of personality development. He can venture an estimate of the level of mastery in psychic growth that has been achieved, the level that remains to be achieved for adequacy, competence, self-realization.

There is bias in Maturational Therapy. The bias includes the belief that implementation of science must be value-rooted. It must reflect ethics and encompass knowledge about society and the direction in which it should be guided. Other facets to the bias are: it is better to be mature than immature; it is better to be autonomous, self-governing than to be enmeshed in intricate, age-inappropriate dependency. It is better to have life directed toward self-fulfillment and self-realization with all of the uncertainties and risks involved than to wallow in the familiar and stagnate. There is firm belief that knowledge is freeing and fleeting; that relationships whether inherited or acquired require investment if they are to be meaningful, enriching.

Central to the thesis of Maturational Therapy is the value of each individual human being. Central, too is the realization that to achieve autonomy, authenticity, openness, trust, involves great risk, great courage and determination.

Theory

It is man's capacity to accumulate substantive knowledge, reflect upon it, synthesize the old and the new that differentiates man from other living creatures. It is man's ability to extrapolate beyond the known through imaginative processes that makes him innovative, the master of his environment. It is true, inaccurate perceptions, invalid feelings may accrue as he grows and can be harbored in the unconscious immune to both the maturation process and rational analysis, interfering often with growth, logical thought and appropriate behavior. This anomaly does not invalidate, does not negate the potency of the conscious, rational processes as an avenue to change in the ongoing life experience.

Many misconceptions, many misconstructions have developed over the years as far as the nature of the human personality is concerned. There was a time when it was believed that one's intelligence was firmly fixed at age 16; that one's personality structure was complete by age 6 and essentially unchangeable. Experience has proved these conceptions, these constructions incorrect. There is evidence that the intelligence is subject to emotional tensions, that it is expandable through experience, through use of mind-expanding drugs. There is ample evidence that personality change is possible at any age via change-inducing processes. History gives dramatic evidence over and over again of man's ability to adapt to changing life conditions. It is erroneous to assume that an individual's rational processes are inoperative just because the coping mechanisms at his command are inadequate to his life situation. This is an assumption we have been making ever since Freud formulated the concept of the unconscious and made a study of it.

In Maturational Therapy the concept of the unconscious is explicit. Sometimes it is referred to as a place, a place in the human structure where forgotten experience, thoughts, feelings are stored. Sometimes the unconscious is spoken of as a person, a despot zealously guarding his domain against the intrusion of reality, reason, logic. Explicit also is the fact that we do not know the channel from the conscious, rational processes to the unconscious. We only know that a channel exists. The unconscious does relinquish its hold. Archaic perceptions, thoughts, feelings do yield to reality, to reason, to logic.

In this respect the psychotherapeutic situation is no different from the medical. The doctor does not know how the body heals. He only knows that given a certain condition, employing certain procedures, it does heal. For the psychotherapist, verbal communication, words, ideas, facts are the chemistry, the surgical instruments of intervention.

Recent research on the physiology of the brain has yielded some most interesting findings.[1] Each of the two hemispheres perform separate, distinctive functions. The left hemisphere seems to specialize in language, logic, analytical thinking; the right seems to be the locus of artistic talent, body awareness and orientation in space. The right side of the brain does not have the capacity for speech. It integrates material in a simultaneous rather than linear pattern. That there is a channel between the two hemispheres is suggested by the fact that what the nonverbal right side of the brain experiences is transmitted to the left side which is capable of verbal expression.

This research might well be moving toward discovery of a

physiological locus of the unconscious. Perhaps it really is a place, a specific area in the brain. Where psychic material stored in the unconscious interferes with logical, rational functioning, the problem may be a blockage in the channel between the left and right sides of the brain. Perhaps what therapy does is whittle away at the blockage—fears, anxiety, insecurity. Hence the need for a sure-footed guide; support, faith that the course is real, that it is manageable, masterable.

In the therapeutic context the unconscious often looms as an enemy rather than an ally, or if not an enemy, at least an obstructive, restricting, inhibiting force. And the individual protests: "I wish my unconscious would listen." Or: "What am I going to do about my unconscious? It doesn't want to hear."

There is an answer to the "What can I do?" It lies in the individual's readiness and ability to take responsibility, his willingness to forego the protection his unconscious is affording him. Perhaps the unconscious is shielding him from facing and dealing with aggressive impulses. Perhaps it is shielding him from worries about castration, impotence, stemming from his aggressive fantasies; his concern that his behavior will get out of control. Perhaps he has invested his unconscious with power because he is afraid. In other words, the power the unconscious holds and wields is power accorded wittingly or unwittingly by the individual. The tenaciousness of the power-hold rests in the individual's unwillingness or inability to take over his own life management.

To divest the unconscious of power involves some very specific tasks. Among these are: acknowledgement that one was once very young; that having been reared in the Western culture nuclear family one has had certain life experiences; that these life experiences invoked fantasies, wishes that were destructive, that from these emerged anxieties, guilt, fears and a very bad sense of self (worries about lovableness, worthwhileness, trustworthiness). These are facts we know about people development in our culture. It is not necessary that the individual be able to recall or reconstruct these events. Nor does he need to remember his feelings of omnipotence, and omniscience, his thoughts of magical power that excited and frightened him. He needs to know the facts but only from an academic point of view, i.e., that they are true for all people in our culture. That for him common realities have somehow become consolidated or fused rather than resolved in the course of time is the problem. Through some psychic mismanagement or miscommunication, realities failed to gain ascendancy over fantasies. A stultifying of the maturational process resulted.

The essential task is not catharsis or eradication. It is rather the clarification of reality, in all of its facets, cognitive, affective operational. It is having reality supplant whatever remains of the archaic in the individual's management of his life experiences and relationships.

Clues to the nature and source of the individual's difficulties are sought in:

The statement of the problem: is it dissatisfaction with self; with others; with the situation

Expectations, stated, implied: are they realistic in terms of himself, others, the situation

Values, stated implied: are they valid

Goals: are they valid, realistic, adequate'

Is the individual struggling with traditional sterotyped thinking in a rapidly changing world? Are his reactions consistent with reality or reflective of unresolved fantasies, invalid fears?

At 40, a mother of three, Mrs. W. protests that nothing she says, thinks, feels meets with the approval of her father. What about her husband? Oh, it had never occurred to her to wonder what he thought.

At 50, married, the father of four, Mr. T was troubled. For the third time he had achieved outstanding success in his business. For the third time he found himself on the verge of bankruptcy. It was not bad planning, or bad judgment. It was simple, stupid carelessness. In correcting the simple, stupid errors he had whittled away all of his profits, all of his equity. He just could not go on this way the rest of his life.

Perceptions

PERSON PERCEPTION

Educators and philosophers seem to be rediscovering or at least stating with new fervor, the view that every individual is a "miracle." Each individual, they assert, writes his own intellectual history. Provided with whatever opportunities you will, he will take out of them what is germane to himself. This is a sobering thought. For the clinician it poses new considerations. Perhaps it was not the individual's childhood that was so bad. Perhaps, instead, the child's image of himself was so bad he could construe life experiences only in their most negative sense. Beth is an excellent case in point. She was a quiet, lovable, obedient child. Her demands were minimal. She seemed to enjoy and appreciate whatever she received. When Beth preferred staying home with her grandmother to going picnicking with the family, her parents assumed it was because she loved her grandmother so. They had no way of knowing that Beth was imposing her own punishment on herself for her wicked thoughts, for her destructive wishes.

Similarly Bob's parents had no way of knowing that Bob's uninterest in toys, in any type of possession, was his way of avoiding punishment, in essence abrogating their authority over him. Their favorite form of punishment had been to deprive him of his favorite toys. He thwarted them most effectively by having nothing that he cared about. Fantasy, his very own mental concoctions which they could not invade substituted for thing-dependent pleasures.

How could anyone possibly know—parents, teachers, friends—that Rick's precipitous withdrawal from learning, from music, from friends had its roots in the fact that he, at age 7, had stolen an eraser from his very best friend. Now at age 15, suddenly realizing his ability for leadership, he panicked. He knew he could do awful things, like stealing and he didn't want the power to hurt!

HUMAN POTENTIALITIES

As personality theorists examine the many different types of intelligence; as biochemists postulate the activation of the $7^{1}/_{2}$ billion brain cells that lie dormant in the human brain, the vision of man's ultimate potential is staggering. This of course is not the common perception of the human being, either on the part of society, or on the part of the human being himself. What a tragedy, one educator lamented, that so many children at ages 6 and 7 already see themselves as failures. What a tragedy indeed. What an indictment of our world; of the adult-child interaction.

One must acknowledge that the human potential comes with no guarantee, no warranty of fulfillment. At the same time, neither does it come with built-in obsolescence. Human potential exists, a part of genetic equipment. It can be activated and developed at any time during the individual's life span. Inhibitors to the realization of potential can be internal. They can be external. In Iron Curtain countries it is doubtful that many options exist for many people. In our own country these past 200 years, options have been circumscribed by the needs of an industrializing society, the need for conformity, for the "man in the gray flannel suit." With the emergence of the postindustrial era, restraints are yielding. Interest is being expressed in job satisfaction not only in production; encouragement of creativity is being heard. In education, the gifted are being recognized as having special needs; the average student is beginning to be viewed as having his own learning rhythm. The rigidity that has characterized education these past hundred years is giving way to programming that acknowledges differences in readiness and aptitude. Education as a lifetime enterprise too is finding its way into social consciousness and being implemented in postcareer programs and in advanced educational programs that operate without campuses or classrooms.

ANOMALIES

At the same time that our highly mobile world, with extended leisure and ever-increasing lifespan provides multiple options, curious phenomena appear. There is what seems to be a mounting preoccupation with sex, the "worm's-eye view" of the universe. Yugoslavian Minister of Welfare Eugen Pusic observed at the International Conference of Social Welfare in 1967 (Washington, D.C.), that when people were faced with freedom of choice among many options, their first reaction was to withdraw.

Perhaps our current preoccupation with sex represents just this phenomenon, a temporary withdrawal, an interim adjustment to the new. Hopefully, on a broad societal level "it too will pass" and we will be ready and able to address ourselves to the phenomenal opportunities that exist and that can give purpose and enrichment to the life experience.

Another curious phenomenon is the holiday pilgrimage home and the centrality this seems to have in the lifestyle of children and parents. Does this signal the indestructibility of the blood tie, a nonseverable umbilical cord? If so, is this genetically determined; sociologically? If it is a genetic reality, how did individuals of earlier generations who left the family fold with no hope or chance of return handle this internal reality? If it is sociologically determined, what is it our current society does to create and perpetuate it? Is this a condition or influence that should be or can be perpetuated in the emerging world? Does the pilgrimage home suggest admiration, affection, love, a sense of duty for and to family? Is it suggestive of an overriding search for the unqualified belonging that only family can give? Family do not have to like you, they do not have to love you but as Robert Frost put it "they have to take you in." There is something secure about that. Is the pilgrimage home merely a "some place to go" in keeping with the on-the-run world of which we are a part? Is it an escape from boredom, from aloneness, loneliness? Is it the line of least resistance? Is it another form of withdrawal from the wide-open world?

TASK PERCEPTION
It is estimated that our society is experiencing the second catastrophic change in human history. The first occurred 5000 years ago, in the shift from primitive to civilized society. Little wonder that the dislocations we are experiencing are so pervasive, so massive. The social institutions that have provided the framework for our society—family, religion, education, marriage, parenthood—are in a state of upheaval. Old patterns are being discarded. New patterns are burgeoning. Everything both old and new is suspect.

There are some clear, persistent questions: Will the institution of marriage survive? If so in what form; to what end? If neither men nor women have to look to marriage for comfort, convenience, security and sex, what will be the function, the reason for being of the long-term, committed relationship? Will marriage provide the "nice place to come home to"? Will it be the core from which and around which other facets of the life experience evolve? What will longevity without aging do to the man-woman relationship; to the experience of parenthood? Will parenthood become only one of many episodes in the total life experience? These questions are certainly unanswerable today. They are questions, the children of today will undoubtedly have to seriously engage.

In the meantime, it is for a fluid, volatile, unsettled life situation, people, whatever their age, must be prepared for today. The therapeutic situation is only one of many arenas in which the preparation can be undertaken.

Three characteristics seem essential for the management of fluidity and flux: (1) autonomy, (2) authenticity, and (3) relatedness.

AUTONOMY

Autonomy in the human personality is self-hood: a sense of separateness, a sense of wholeness, integrity, internal security. With autonomy comes: increased accuracy in the perception of reality (people, things, situations); less dependence upon the familiar, more curiosity and challenge in the unfamiliar, the unknown. The autonomous individual knows his limitations. He feels guilty only about those things which he should and could change but chooses not to. His behavior, attitudes, reactions are guided by his own values and goals, not by conventionality. He accepts rituals as a part of the enrichment of life not as mandatory of constricting. They are subject to his free choice.[2]

The autonomous individual can be alone without being lonely. He can learn from anyone who has something to teach, whether he likes or is liked by that person. He can be angry but his anger will be reality-related rather than a reaction contaminated by fantasy, fear, anxiety, prejudice. It is in the doing that he derives satisfaction. Success is not essential to his sense of achievement.

In other words autonomy provides an inner rootedness, a wholeness with which one can move into and out of situations and relationships as reality demands. It does not eliminate the experiencing of loss, and discomfort with change and dislocation. It means only that one can manage it and move on as the life situation requires.

AUTHENTICITY

Approximately thirty years ago, sociologists introduced the role theory. They promoted the view that people were function-dominated, controlled, directed. People played roles. This view of the human personality abrogates authenticity, genuineness, reality. Little wonder that anomie, rootlessness, the absence of a firm sense of self have become a source of concern in our society.

A return to the intrinsics of the human personality seems long overdue. We need to view the human being as multidimensional. We need to view the tasks he performs not in terms of "role" but in terms of the specific dimensions of his personality the task taps. It is the person, his perceptions, his beliefs, his operational pattern that determines how and with what level of efficiency and expertness he performs. Educators are proposing that schools of the future will have as a major task discovering the individual's real strengths—aptitudes, interest, talents—and developing them. This would be a major step in the development of authenticity. The English describe therapy as "sorting oneself out" a perception well worth considering.

For adults seeking to find their way in the morass of the unforeseen, the unpredictable, the task is complex. If one asks oneself: "Will the real me please speak up," there is a tremendous risk. Which of one's committed relationships will stand up in the light of truth: Will anyone like me, or even put up with me? Will I like any of the people who have been important in my life? These are frightening propositions. Dissatisfaction with the current reality must be great or the promise of change very inviting to undertake the task of self-discovery. It can be undertaken, it can be achieved at any age; at any stage of one's life experience and with promise of increased self-realization and self-fulfillment.

RELATEDNESS

Autonomy and authenticity pertain to the self as separate from others. Relatedness concerns the self in the social context. How does the individual move in and out of social contacts; what does he give; what does he receive; what does he expect? The goal is that he be able to move into and out of relationships, whether of long or short duration, appropriately; and that his relationships be based not on psychic need (inability to be alone) but on psychic desire (the wish for enrichment, fulfillment).

Relationships, of course, are manifold, and diverse. They require different levels of involvement. They may even involve different dimensions of personality. There are the relationships that come with the genes: parents, siblings, uncles, aunts, cousins. There are the relationships that come contractually: in-laws. The inherited and the contractually built-in have a quality of mandatoriness in them. They are not subject to free choice. One may choose to be free of them but one pays a price in anxiety and guilt; a price that often diminishes one's own sense of worth. There are relationships that come built-in with other situations—school, work. They also may not be subject to free choice, but choosing to be free of them does not carry the psychic price of those mentioned above. There are the relationships one maintains "for old time's sake." Then there are the optional preferred relationships, the relationships one chooses, cherishes, pursues, promotes for the enrichment, the fulfillment they bring to one's life experience. Marriage ought to stand out boldly in this category. It rarely does. The contract with its "must" and its traditional, "until death do us part" stipulation (spoken or implied) seems all too often to divest marriage early of the specialness in relationship that led to the long-term commitment. Marriage is seen in terms of comfort, convenience, security and sex, rather than in terms of its being a very privileged relationship warranting and requiring a high-level, continuing investment of time, energy, interest on the part of both parties. One may anticipate that in a highly mobile world, with extended leisure, with longevity sans aging, the institution of marriage in its traditional sense is not likely to survive if the psychological dimension of the man-woman relationship does not achieve a higher level of development than it enjoys today.

In addition to the personality characteristics described as autonomy, authenticity, relatedness, the individual needs also a repertoire of psychic tools with which to deal with the life experience in which he finds himself. Among these are:

1. a clear concept of reality: what is possible and impossible, what is and is not feasible
2. clarity about others: their abilities, their limitations
3. ability to learn: openness, curiosity, imagination; freedom from anxiety about each
4. ability to trust
5. knowledge: what is happening in the world that might account for his distress; that might hold promise for the future

GOAL PERCEPTION

Goals in Maturational Therapy are as differential, as varied as in any other therapeutic scheme. Similarly, the determinants of goals are differential and varied. There are the exigencies of reality (what is possible given a set of circumstances). There is the intent and determination of the applicant (what he wants and what he is willing to invest to achieve it; this may be in terms of money, time, energy, discomfort). There is the skill of the practitioner, including his goal-perception. There are practitioners, for instance, who think primarily in terms of stress alleviation. There are those whose focus is on adaptation to reality. There are others who think in terms of the potential of the individual, what would bring him to self-realization and strive to help him understand and work toward achieving this. Often the individual in distress has no idea of the source of his problem or the levels of change that are available to him. Here the assessment capacity and perception of the practitioner is of crucial importance both at the onset of treatment in setting possible goals and as treatment progresses.

With the perception of people as thinking, adaptable, growing, changing, movement in the direction of greater self-fulfillment, greater self-realization can take place at any time. This perception introduces hope. It introduces challenge. It places the individual in a position of responsibility for the direction of his life, within the potentials that are available to him, internally, externally.

Climate and Procedures

Maturational Therapy as herein described involves no game playing, no special terminology. Since the search is for essence, for authenticity the operational format between therapist and the individual seeking help is: You are you. I am I. You have problems; I have knowledge, skills, experience. Let us see whether together we can undertake the task and achieve the goals appropriate to your needs and desires. There are no preliminaries. A simple: "What can I do for you?" sets the stage for explication, inquiry, interaction, intervention.

The procedures vary. If the statement of the problem is amorphous, without focus, information on onset of the problem or concern about a problem might be sought as well as information on the timing of the request for help. If the problem is specific— inability to learn; marital infidelity; sexual compulsiveness; social ineptness, specific intervention is undertaken to bring the problem into the reality focus of option-cost and engage the individual consciously in the change process.

Option-Cost Format

For the student, whatever his age and stage in the learning situation, the reality is he doesn't have to learn. Why is it that inability to learn is causing him distress? Is it the risk of parental and societal disapproval? Is it realization that without learning his own life goals, or the goals he thinks he wants will not be realizable? This is an important determination. It involves consideration of his rights as an individual vis-à-vis the rights of others to impose their goals, desires, standards upon him. The therapist is prepared to become the individual's ally helping him achieve the goals of his choice, helping him deal with the external forces that interfere with this: the disappointment, disapproval of parents, peers, society. The therapist is prepared to provide external affirmation of the self whatever that self may be. There is one major condition here, the individual's goals must be consistent with the therapist's basic moral values.

For instance, a 19-year-old, extremely bright but completely nonfunctioning struggled with the possibility of directing his talents to becoming a skilled criminal. This would have been possible as far as his psychic organization was concerned. He could have attained skill but not success, i.e., he was more likely to be caught and spend much of his time in jail. The war between a strong superego imparted by his mother and a strong impulse to deviance suppressed in his father was intense. Whether the conflict was within the realm of conscious, rational control was unknown. What was made clearly known was that if the individual chose the antisocial course of action, the therapist was not the person to help him. She could not and would not tolerate antisocial behavior. He had to make a choice: would he, could he keep his antisocial impulses under control? If so, the therapist would be glad to try to help him resolve the problems that were interfering with his use of his intellectual potential. If not, he would have to find another therapist. He decided on the former. To demonstrate the seriousness of his intent and the extent of his determination, he decided to return some stolen merchandise, considering in detail beforehand what the possible price of such an action might be. He followed through and though the temptation to deviance recurred sporadically, he managed successfully to control it and treatment proceeded.

Should the therapist's willingness to help the individual become what he presumably wishes to be, be disparate with what the individual believes he should want, explosive anger might result, an overt expression of "who needs you"? "If I wanted to be what I want to be I wouldn't be here." The conflict is clear: Do I have a right to be what I want to be if that is not consistent with my parents' wishes or society's standards? Yes, you have a right to be whatever you want to be. There is a price for each option. What options are open to you? What price is involved in each? For you to have your preference what must you achieve?

The essence in this clarification is an incontrovertible reality: Each individual can be only what he can be. There are the outer limits of genetic potential: intellectual, affective, motor. There are the acquired inhibitors. An individual whose capacity for relationship was damaged during the first six months of his life through the absence of a sustaining, nurturing adult, is not likely to be able to engage in an intensive, sustained therapeutic relationship. A woman who has not resolved her penis envy by the age of six or seven is likely to have difficulty using her maximum potential in any enterprise because of deeply buried worries about her aggressive impulses that might get out of control. A person who has not mastered the oedipal situation is not likely to be able to sustain success in any endeavor, learning, work, relationships. A child of a promiscuous mother faces a phenomenally difficult task if she prefers to thwart her own tendency to sexual compulsiveness and use her energies and talents in more socially acceptable ways.

There are limits to the rational control of behavior. A young woman might want desperately to become a doctor, and to have the intellectual wherewithal to do so. In her way is her unconscious, the reservoir of unresolved castration fantasies, the wish for her brother's penis compounded and confounded by stereotyped societal patterns of gender-determined activities: men are supposed to be the doctors, engineers, mechanics; girls, the nurses, teachers, salespeople.

The limits must be acknowledged, clarified. In other words, it is important that the individual seeking help have affirmation immediately that the situation in which he finds himself is "known," as are the conditions that create it. Known, also, are the procedures by which the situation can be altered.

The realities are both implicit and explicit in the therapeutic process: (1) the therapist is in control of the treatment procedure; (2) the individual is in control of his involvement in the treatment situation. His is the ultimate authority, i.e., to proceed or not, but in exercising that authority he must be responsible. One might go so far as to say that he has the right to hurt himself, but he does not have the right to compromise the therapeutic situation through indecisiveness. This is made clear from the very beginning.

The saddest situation of my almost 40 years in social work involved a 19-year-old, unusually bright, exceptionally innovative. In the third interview she made what seemed to be the considered decision to proceed with treatment. The source of her problem seemed clear. The treatment procedure, also. In the fourth interview, she sat on the edge of the chair firmly clutching her coat as though afraid someone would snatch it from her. She had made a decison. She would not continue. All of her life, all of her relationships had been based on her problems. She did not know how she could possibly manage without them. I was terribly sorry. Her potentials were so great. Her problems would interfere with her realizing them. This was not unusual, but it always made me sad. There was just the barest trace of ambivalence as she listened: if she withdrew now, would anyone, at any time be able to help her. Of course, I affirmed without qualification. She was highly treatable. Any time she decided she wanted to change she could. The problem would be to find a therapist in whom she had confidence, whom she could trust with the authority, the power to invade her established patterns of behavior and relationships. I never saw her, or heard from her again.

Investigations into the operations of the mind are yielding information pertinent to the clinician. One finding is the importance of "mental set." Of a group of individuals who were told to remember nonsense syllables, twice as many remembered as those who were not alerted to the task. Other findings include: Unless one is trained to listen one hears only 25 percent of the time; emotions heighten perceptions. A person who is afraid will be preoccupied with noises another person does not hear. Once our brains have been fed information, rest is necessary for assimilation of the data and possibly for reorganization of it into new thoughts, new insights. Researchers have found that the best ideas emerge in periods of relaxation, often as one is falling asleep. Researchers at the Langley-Porter Institute have found that the capacity for insight development can be systematically improved. What must be developed is the ability to see what is, instead of what one would wish, a willingness to examine what is and what might be. This is difficult because we tend to avoid what is unfamiliar, what takes effort. The efficiency of the brain is affected by blood circulation which can be improved through exercise and by food which serves as its fuel.[3]

In Maturational Therapy a "mental set" is established: (1) there is a problem; (2) there are procedures through which the problem can be resolved; (3) there are conditions necessary for effective use of the procedures.

Structure and Conditions of Treatment

The format which I have found useful and effective has been as follows: (1) If the individual wishes to proceed beyond the first interview, there must be a minimum of four, inclusive. (2) These four interviews constitute the diagnostic period, the period during which the individual determines whether I can be helpful; I consider whether he is using our discussions well. (3) At the end of the four interviews we both assess what has been achieved and what more, if anything, remains to be done. Assuming that the task that remains to be done is within the therapist's range of competence, the decision to continue or discontinue rests with the individual. Beyond the four interviews, the therapist makes clear it is impossible for her to give a time estimate. This will depend on the level of achievement the individual wishes to attain, minimal (symptom-free), moderate (adaptation, behavioral modification), maximal (reconstruction: mastery of unresolved maturational tasks; realization of maximum potential). It will depend also on the amount of interference the unconscious exerts in the treatment process.

There are many plateaus along the way at which the individual can stop. Only one condition is imposed: Should the individual decide to stop at a point not mutually agreed upon, he agrees to come in for one final interview. The reason for this is that the therapist wishes to make available to the individual every step of the way the best of her knowledge and skill. She does not want to be deterred from moving in or ahead for fear the individual in a state of intense anxiety might decide to withdraw. The one final interview affords the opportunity to insure that maximum gain from the treatment experience is protected.

In actuality, this mandatory final interview is rarely necessary. The therapist inured to the will-counterwill dynamic is extremely sensitive to ambivalence. Tardiness on the part of a person usually prompt, broken appointments (differentiated from substituted appointents), expressions of futility and hopelessness, redundancy, each suggest vacillation, a reduction in the determination to change. This is brought into the discussion as soon as it is perceived by the therapist. It is clarified and acted upon. The mandatory last interview is rarely necessary. Only recently when I was taking responsibility for terminating in the light of recurrent ambivalence and resistance, the individual reminded me that he had made a commitment to see me beyond his decision to terminate, one extra interview. He wanted to hold me to that commitment. He knew he was being resistive. He knew he was ambivalent. But that had been the pattern of all of his life and all of his relationships. He was not sure that terminating treatment was right. That might be true, I acknowledged.

But one thing I would not permit was that he place me in a position of irresponsibility. Each time he had recommitted himself to treatment I had accepted that as firm. Each time we proceeded and progress was made, the ambivalence and resistance recurred. After three abortive commitments with the end of treatment clearly in sight, I had to conclude that the current ambivalence represented resistance to further mastery of the maturational tasks necessary for realization of maximum potential. It seemed to me what he was saying was he is grown up enough for now. That is fine. Final decision was deferred until after a two-week vacation. The decision at this writing remains in balance.

Content: Substantive

Another aspect of "mental set" employed in Maturational Therapy is substantive content. Two major categories of content are used: (1) objective knowledge: what is known about personality development as it pertains to the problems about which the individual is concerned; and (2) corrective concepts: the issues of "love," "musts," "rights."

OBJECTIVE KNOWLEDGE
Most often in the discussion of causative factors in the presenting problems, reference is made to that period of personality development when the child struggles with his sexuality (how come he does or she doesn't have a penis), with the oedipal situation, with worries about magical power and about impulses getting out of control. This material is presented as knowledge—every child reared in the Western culture, nuclear family is subject to these

experiences. There is nothing abnormal, pathological about them. The problems the individual is having suggest only that he did not successfully resolve or master the experiences. The reasons for this usually rest in the child's life situation or in his relationships. Often parents inadvertently, unwittingly reinforce childhood fantasies instead of helping the child master them.

The therapeutic process does not require that the childhood experiences be expurgated. They cannot be. Their imprint on the individual's life experience and personality are indelible. What is hoped is that via the therapeutic process the destructive effects of the childhood experiences can be expunged and the individual freed to realize his maximum potential, whatever that might be.

CORRECTIVE CONCEPTS

There are a number of misconceptions current in our society that impede the maturational process and inhibit the full enjoyment of life. Among them is the fantasy of "love," the fantasy of the ever-present, unqualified, unlimited, all-encompassing relationship. It did exist once for all human beings, i.e., in the womb. Then all needs, wishes, desires were met without request, without even conscious awareness of need or desire. The longing for that apparently blissful state seems to be present in everyone to a greater or lesser degree. To whatever degree it exists it is destined to frustration. For the all-encompassing love does not exist—one human being to another.

By the same token love is not a "right." It does not come with the genes. One cannot be sure that the persons who gave one birth are equipped or inclined to love. Love cannot be demanded, or legislated. Where it develops it carries with it no warranty, no guarantee as to intensity, adequacy, length of time. Love at very best is fragile. It can be easily injured, shattered. It can survive injury but not without scars. Too often, people look to marriage for the love that was unsatisfied in the parent-child relationship, the nurturing, the forgiving. The umbilical cord is biologically severable to be sure. Psychological severing is much more complex. It has been achieved rarely in our society and then with much guilt. Society has invested the parent-child relationship with characteristics and quality immune to reason, immune to practicality. It has attempted to do the same with marriage and for a number of centuries virtually succeeded. But times are changing radically now. It is not possible to know at this point whether the fluidity that is developing in the relationship between men and women will generalize to the relationship between biological parents and offspring. A major concern in our society today is what will happen to children of unstructured, transitory unions. This remains to be seen.

Another misconception is that of the "musts." The "musts," the "I have to's" which people accept or contrive for themselves are many and varied. Rarely, if ever, in the population that seeks help does one find what recent songs have asserted: "I've got to be me"; or I've got to do it "my way." These are the surgings of youth. It is too early to know the results of this self-assertion, these attempts at self-affirmation.

A playwright many years ago posed that there are two "musts": one must pay taxes and one must die. The current reality is that one does not have to pay taxes, one can go to jail. One does still have to die. If the scientific projection materializes, by the year 2091, immortality will be a choice the human being will have. Cell regeneration will maintain the body at age 25. The brain will continue to develop ad infinitum. Then there will be no "musts." Full responsibility for choice will lie with each person.

In place of "musts" emerge options; and each option carries a price, a price in time, effort, frustration; a price possibly in comfort, security, relationships. For effective choice one needs certain equipment. One needs to have some idea of who one is: what one likes, what one dislikes; what brings one pleasure; what yields displeasure. One needs to have some idea of what one would like to do with one's life experience, i.e., have some goals. And one needs some clarity on values: what is important; what unimportant. These will be the issues that will determine what the individual will be willing to invest in his life experience. Thence will emerge the options he will choose.

In order to be a free agent in the option-cost situation an individual needs also to be clear on rights: his right to be who he is, to become what he can and chooses to be. He has a right to be wrong, he has a right to make mistakes, to forgive himself and to be forgiven for them.

There is still another right which is extremely difficult for us to acknowledge because of our firm grounding in the puritan ethic. That is the right to do nothing; to be nothing. It is a right by default, i.e., because it cannot be denied. "You can lead a horse to water but you can't make him drink," is the way the old adage goes. What holds for horses, holds for people too. One can provide a vast array of experiences and opportunities, the individual cannot be forced to avail himself of them.

Perhaps the greatest challenge to the clinician is the individual of superior intelligence and innovative capacity who is nonfunctioning, or functioning on a minimal level. What often operates is not lack of incentive or lack of motivation. These individuals frequently have high-level goals well within their ability. What is inhibiting is unresolved fantasies of omnipotence and omniscience characteristic of the 3-year-old, and anxieties about aggression stemming from the destructive wishes, and the imagined magical power, residues of the oedipal situation.

Acknowledging to these individuals their right not to use the equipment with which nature endowed them and at the same time acknowledging waste that such a course entails for themselves, for others is a first step in the process of engagement. The next is clarifying the roots of the problem and the third step is the assurance that the roots are excisable; the forces inhibiting their maximum performance and self-realization are irradicable. What one seeks to affirm is the individual's right to fulfillment of his highest potential and the fact that this can be made possible. What the individual has to decide is: Does he want to be different; is he willing to be involved in, to invest in the change process. In other words his right "to be" and "to become" carries the price of responsibility and involvement.

Implicit in the acknowledgement and affirmation of one's own rights, is the acknowledgement and affirmation of the rights of others. Implicit in it also is the realization that one's power to control is limited to control over and of oneself. For instance there is no way that we can determine or control how another person thinks, feels, acts. We can react, i.e., we can approve, disapprove, like, dislike, accept, reject what the other person says or does, but we cannot affect it; nor do we have the right to expect or demand that he change. We have the prerogative only to act in response to it. The prevalence of the idea that we can or should be able to control how other people react is an indication of how prevalent and persistent are the residuals of childhood, the fantasies of omnipotence. It is amazing how rare it is to find individuals who understand, accept and respond in accordance with the reality that each person is separate, an entity unto himself, and entitled to that separateness and responsible for it.

One cannot deny an irascible man his ill-temperedness. One can point out the effect of his behavior on others and the price he pays for his lack of control. One can refuse to be a party to it or a victim of it. He then must make the choice to continue or modify his reaction.

Conclusion

Maturational Therapy accentuates the positive: the human potential for growth, modification, transformation. It pursues and capitalizes upon the innate human characteristic: the striving for self-fulfillment. Its requirements are stringent. They include: (1) the commitment to change; to want change even if you don't want it (everyone indulges the fantasy, the wish that he can have what he wants "as is;" change at best is second best); (2) Maturational Therapy requires that the individual be ready and able to engage in a sustained relationship; (3) that he be ready and able to invest the therapist with the authority, the power to invade, intervene in his established patterns of thought, feeling, behavior; and (4) it requires that he be ready and able to manage the disquietude that accompanies the change process.

Levels of achievement are determined primarily by the individual, his intent, his determination. The therapist has the opportunity and the responsibility to spell out the potentials, to help the individual learn to want (both learning and wanting are acquired responses; they do not come with the genes). The ultimate choice of goals remains with the individual. Some are content with reduced symptoms, identified as the lowest rung of the maturational ladder. Some seek improvement in functioning and in lifestyle. Some are content only if they reach the highest rung of the treatment ladder.

Built into the treatment situation early are three facts: (1) treatment cannot guarantee specific results; it cannot guarantee that there will be a marriage, for instance, or that the talented individual will be able to maximize his talents; (2) the hope is that through treatment the individual will become clear as to his options and his rights and that he will be free to engage both; (3) the ultimate success of treatment rests with the individual, his taking responsibility. Old behaviors will always remain available. Responsibility for choice of the old or the new remains irrevocably with the individual. He ultimately determines the success of treatment.

Notes

1. Ornstein, Robert E., "Right and Left Thinking," *Psychology Today* (May 1973).
2. Levitas, G. B., *The World of Psychology* (New York: Braziller, 1963).
3. Deutsch, Patricia and Ron, "Are You Making the Most of Your Mind?", *Family Circle* (April 1967), p. 38.

Bibliography

Erikson, Erik, *Identity, Youth and Crisis* (New York: Norton, 1968).
Ford, Donald, and Urban, Hugh, *Systems of Psychotherapy* (New York: Wiley, 1965).
Glasser, William, *Reality Therapy* (New York: Harper & Row, 1965).
Harris, Thomas, *I'm O.K.—You're O.K.* (New York: Avon, 1963).
The Humanist, various issues.
Intellectual Digest, various issues.
LeVine, Robert, *Culture, Behavior, Personality* (Chicago: Aldine, 1973).
Maslow, A. H., "Self-Actualization: A Study in Psychological Health," *Symposia on Topical Issues*, vol. I (New York: Grune & Stratton, 1950).
Psychology Today, various issues.
Saturday Review, various issues.
Toffler, Alvin, *Future Shock* (New York: Bantam, 1971).
World, various issues.

CHAPTER 3

Comprehensive National Health Insurance: What It May Mean to the Mental Health Practitioner*

Every end is a beginning. The end is where we start from.
                                                    T. S. Eliot

Prologue

We are about to witness the terminal phases of some of our most persistent social and psychological constructs. Economic poverty which has been with us for centuries is about to give way to the guaranteed annual wage or the negative income tax. The "captured" clientele inherent in the traditional social agency structure is about to give way to the freelance consumer in the open market of mental health intervention. Being taken "on faith" is fast being replaced by a "proof of the pudding," "I'm from Missouri" mental set. Immunity from critical appraisal, immunity from fault which experts have enjoyed in the past is no more. Everyone, no matter what his status or his stature is subject to question; everyone may be called to account.

* Presented at the 15th Annual I-CAPP Conference, Toronto, June 29, 1976.

- Consumers are suing chairmen of boards in industry for faulty products.
- A parent sued a board of education because his son, a high school graduate, could not read.
- The AMA is challenging HEW for authorizing nonmedical personnel to make medical decisions.
- Doctors are suing insurance companies for settling malpractice suits out of court thereby implying guilt.
- One parent posed to educators the question: "If you can teach a chimpanzee to read why not my retarded child?"

Indeed this last question may be asked of many other professions in many other contexts. Some theorists venture that it will no longer be acceptable to say that an individual cannot change. The onus will be on the intervener to develop the methods, the techniques, the procedures that will produce the desired results.

Chaotic is how it feels. Chaotic it is. Alvin Toffler suggests that the shift from an industrial to a postindustrial society is equivalent to the first "catastrophic" change in human history—the shift from primitive to civilized society 5000 years ago. If this is so we must prepare for an extensive period of dislocation and disruption as: (1) familiar institutions disappear; (2) established values are subjected to critical scrutiny; (3) traditional guidelines no longer guide.

The inexpertness of experts in predicting, directing, controlling change is disillusioning. It gives impetus to the anitiintellectual, antiknowledge forces which have surfaced in recent years. That our current level of knowledge is not adequate to the current scope and rate of change should spur us to extending our knowledge not to retreating from it.

It is not likely that anything will halt the change that is in process and in progress. Historians, philosophers, theoreticians tell us we can affect the course and the outcome of change. Here lies the challenge. Do we choose to address ourselves to it? I am hoping that as we meet together in Toronto (I-CAPP '76), our answer will be firmly in the affirmative. It is to this end that I present my view of the challenge; and enlist your participation.

Two thoughts guide my deliberations: From George B. Leonard:

Not to dream boldly may turn out to be simply irresponsible.

From Rene Dubois:

The next fifty years must not be an extrapolation of today but an original model of life that seeks qualitative change rather than quantitative growth and with a more humane, original approach to life.

Directional Signals

Emerging Realities

PSYCHOLOGICAL POVERTY

If and when economic poverty fades into history much as did the dodo bird and the dinosaur, we may expect a new kind of poverty to surface—psychological. Evidence of psychological poverty is already abundant in (1) the increasing number of suicides among youth and most highly educated—an international phenomenon; (2) the number of people in mental institutions; (3) the amount of money being spent on tranquilizers and energizers in our most affluent, best-educated populations; (4) the number of people who resort to alcohol and drugs for relaxation, recreation and for coping.

Our society cannot afford to lose to death, illness, drugs its most promising members. If in the area of democratic ideals our society hopes for the world leadership it has achieved in the industrial and economic spheres, it must make available to all of its members the opportunity for self-realization, whatever the capacity for self-realization may be.

THE OPEN MARKET

Heinz has its 57 varieties of relishes, Howard Johnson has its 28 flavors of ice cream. Mental health is fast approaching an equally varied, enticing prospectus. There are therapists of many persuasions. There are procedures to suit the taste or whet the appetite of the most conservative and the most venturesome. Consumers are free to shop (even window-shop), to test, to change. The hazards are great; much greater when one is dealing with psychic forces than with gastronomic. This is so because we know very little about the psychic forces, their tolerance limits, their potentials. Also, consumers have few guidelines to help them distinguish between the qualified practitioner and the charlatan, the faddist, the gimmick-vendor. There are groups, there are books, there are movies that should include in their captions: "This may prove hazardous to your mental health." At least this would alert the individual to the fact that the psyche, not only the body, is vulnerable to destructive influence.

An Insurance-Based Service System

It is projected that by 1978–79, a mandatory comprehensive health insurance program will be in effect. Mental health services will be included in the coverage. Taking the Senator Edward Kennedy Bill #S3286 and Representative Wilbur Mills #H.R. 13870 as a prototype one finds provisions of particular significance to those involved in mental health intervention.

1. That health maintenance as well as treatment be provided.
2. Where there are physical disorders requiring hospitalization, there is no limit to the hospital stay. Stays in a psychiatric hospital are limited to "30 days of active treatment and 60 days of partial hospitalization for mental illness per year."
3. Where home health care is necessary there is recommended 100 days of service. For out-patient mental illness services are "limited to the estimated cost of 30 such visits with a private practitioner in a comprehensive community care center; half that amount is the cost limit if services are performed in any other setting."*
4. That professional providers would be reimbursed on the basis of a "fee schedule of reasonable and customary charges."

* American Hospital Association, *Analyses of National Health Insurance Proposals*, 1974, pp. 52–60.

5. That private insurance carriers will be permitted to sell supplementary insurance coverage.
6. That the consumer is free to go to "any individual health care provider" whether that provider is a participant in the national health program or not.

As one considers the vast difference in coverage for physical and psychological disorders one cannot help but be struck with how inadequate, inept perhaps nonexistent have been our efforts in behalf of mental health intervention. Where did the idea of 30 or even 60 days in a mental hospital come from? Certainly not from an analysis of experience. Similarly, where did the estimate of 30 outpatient visits come from? Certainly not from any objective agency experience. This is token representation. Tokenism where mental health intervention is concerned may well prove to be more damaging than no representation. Where psychological anomalies are concerned what can we hope to do, what dare we undertake to do in 30, or at the most 60 interviews? These are serious considerations for the practitioner; for the consumer.

Since the proposals for mandatory comprehensive national health insurance are still in embryo is there something we as an organization or we as individuals might do to achieve more adequate coverage for mental health maintenance and intervention?

There are other issues to which we are alerted by the medical profession's experiences with Medicare, Medicaid and maternal and child care programs. It is not likely that where national health insurance is concerned less will be expected of the mental health practitioner than is being expected of medical personnel. The Professional Standards Review Organization (PSRO) provides the guidelines.

First, one must qualify to participate. The practitioner and/or agency must qualify as vendor. The insured must qualify as consumer. The service must qualify as intervention. Proposed as the qualifying instrument is the *Profile*. There will need to be an Institution Profile, a Practitioner Profile, a Consumer Profile and a Service Profile. The following will give consideration to all but the Institution Profile.

The Practitioner Profile

Hopefully, the Practitioner Profile will require an educational and experiential baseline. This would be objective and verifiable. It would be the simplest dimension and only the beginning of the qualifying procedure for the practitioner.

In a period prolific with innovation such as we are experiencing there is the problem of standards. PSRO defines standards as dealing with "the range of acceptable variation from a norm or criterion." Acceptable to whom might be a pertinent question.

> An individual finds one of the newer techniques helpful. He requests that the practitioner be paid by national health insurance. The technique the practitioner uses is new. It has not been tested. How is the qualifying body to assess if the service qualifies for insurance coverage?

> Perhaps the intervention results only in symptom substitution. Is a lesser symptom a valid achievement? Perhaps the intervention yields only short-term relief of discomfort. Is that acceptable intervention? Perhaps the intervention effected no change because the consumer chose not to use the new options available to him. Is the service to be covered?

Also, having relevance for the Practitioner Profile is the consumer rights movement. Up until very recently service professionals—physicians, attorneys, educators, social workers—were viewed as capable of doing only good. They could not hurt. With the realization that interventions can be good or bad, helpful or hurtful has come the end of immunity from fault. Thanks to Ralph Nader's efforts to establish the locus of responsibility no matter how complex, diffuse, illusive the system no one is immune from accountability; from charges of malpractice, malfeasance. Some chairmen of boards of education are already carrying malpractice insurance for they are being charged with responsibility if students fail to learn. It is possible that every agency executive and board chairman will need to do likewise if they are held responsible for the outcome of services under their jurisdiction. For the practitioner, malpractice insurance may well become a must as they face the issue of accountability no longer protected by the organization for which they work; for the organization itself is accountable and vulnerable. Even if the "no fault" concept is extended to mental health intervention (the consumer is reimbursed for damages without the establishment of negligence, etc.), monitoring and assessment of practitioner performance is certain to be a part of the procedure with special attention to those practitioners whose performance is brought into question.

How can the practitioner reserve the right, enjoy the privilege and fulfill the responsibility of innovation without the risk of being considered a charlatan, a faddist, a gimmick-vendor?

I propose two ways, each of which I believe should be represented in the Practitioner Profile. The first is theoretical:

1. What personality theory or theories guides the practice?
2. What change dynamics do the procedures employed call into play?
3. What are the goals of treatment in each unit of service undertaken?

The second is operational:

1. What are the units of service being provided: central supplementary, peripheral?
2. What are the conditions necessary to provide the service (setting—group, individual; frequency and length of contacts; number of interviews necessary—minimum, median, maximum)?
3. What are the risks (Informed consent is likely to be requisite for service.)?
4. What are the criteria for assessing outcome?

The Service Profile

The mental health practitioner has not been trained to think in terms of "units of service." He has no typology equivalent to the medical professions' organ-related delineations—tonsilectomy, appendectomy, etc. Neither are mental health interventions as identifiable as medical—chemical, nutritional, surgical.

Our knowledge of brain functioning is minimal, elementary. (Only recently have psychologists undertaken to study the processes that operate in the unconscious.) There is no unified personality theory. The dynamics of change that have been identified and the procedures of intervention that have been developed have no specific reference points. They do not pinpoint the dimension of personality they aim to tap. Poorly equipped though we are as far as intellectual skills are concerned and with virtually no practical instruments, we face a monumental task if we are to qualify to participate in an insurance-based service system that will demand accountability, quality control, efficiency and economy.

And time is short. Some of our experienced colleagues maintain that it cannot be done. This may be true. If so, social workers are an "endangered species": subject to extinction because of inability to adapt. Some of us would like to make a bid for a place in the emerging world that will demand accountability, quality control, efficiency, effectiveness. We see this as adding to our strength and to our potential as change-agents. Perhaps we in I-CAPP can make some inroads on the monumental task that faces our profession. The "musts" are clear:

- We must translate the multiproblem situation into "units of service."
- We must estimate for each unit of service a time range: minimum, median, maximum. If the medical model prevails we may anticipate that insurance coverage will be based on a certain percentile of the average or median time usually required for a given condition or circumstance.
- We must be prepared to stipulate projected goals and periodically to estimate the extent to which the goals have been realized.

Because of the nature of the psyche it is important that the assessment procedures include consideration of serendipity, the treatment bonus, the unexpected achievement, the secondary gains.

In the Service Profile there must be flexibility. There must be allowance for the vagaries of the human psyche. The precipitant (the event leading to the request for service), the presenting problem (the issue as the individual sees it) may or may not be central.

It may or may be not be the point at which intervention is necessary or possible.

There must be allowance of the "tip of the iceberg" nature of human perception especially in time of stress.

A mother distraught to the point of immobilization by the out-of-control behavior of her 7-year-old, had given no thought to the possibility that her intolerable marriage might be at the root of the problem.

A father panicked by an almost uncontrollable impulse to kill his son had no inkling he was reacting to the double tragedy in his own life—the death of both parents in one week.

Allowance must be made for fluidity, movement from the obvious to the underlying; from the immediate to the long range.

Ideally, mental health intervention should be viewed as a capital investment in the individual, in all of those who make up his world and in society. The ever widening circle-effect of successful mental health intervention is the compound interest on the capital investment.

Mental health maintenance, protection and promotion should be an integral part of our service structure. Mental health check-ups should be routine at points in the life cycle known to entail high level stress: marriage, parenthood, graduation, etc. Mental health epidemics such as the suicide epidemic rampant in our society today should be acknowledged, and minutely examined for the causative agents, not swept under the rug or relegated to the skeleton closet. How to protect oneself from suicide should be taught just as one is taught how to avoid agents that bring diseases to the body.

Another part of the challenge is the development of incentives and instruments to good mental health. There is already on the market a medical insurance that reimburses the insured at the end of each year that he has not been ill. There have been societies that have reimbursed physicians when their patients have remained well, not when they have been ill. Such a refocusing and reordering may well be among the possibilities we face.

The Consumer Profile

It has been estimated that as of 1975, 70 percent of the population over 25 years of age in the U.S. will have had at least a high school education. They will have learned the skills of critical evaluation, creative imagination and conceptualization. Continuing knowledge is not only readily available. It is difficult to avoid. The mass media are on constant alert to what is new, different with little regard for validity, feasibility, end result. Instancy is the expectation. Instancy is featured and fostered. Instant coffee, the short-order meal generalizes to instant, short-order solutions, relationships, love. This new population is not likely to be content with being "not ill." They are more likely to think in terms of "the best of health" and as a "right."

Historically, mental health intervention has followed the medical model with its focus on malfunctioning and pathology. The physical body of the human species is an impressive organism. A clue to its complexity is found in the fact that there are 100,000 symptoms and only 10,000 known diseases. The psyche is even more complex.

Webster defines the psyche or mind as "an organic system reaching all parts of the body and serving to adjust the total organism to the needs or demands of the environment." It is estimated that there are 15 billion brain cells, that only half of these are activated and that the most accomplished human beings use only 5–10 percent of the activated brain cells.

Psychologists claim to have isolated 70 different intelligences and estimate that there may be 50 more (what they mean by "intelligences" has not been specified). It has been estimated that there are 20 personality theories, 13 dynamics of change and 52 treatment procedures (again, without specification).* Chemical intervention has already succeeded in restoring at least to some extent brain functioning impaired by vascular accidents. It has succeeded in increasing within limits the intellectual capacity of retarded children, and bringing aggressive behavior under con-

* See Appendix for my attempt at specification.

trol. It may well be that chemistry may be the solution to prejudice. Animal research suggests it may also be an instrument for learning. The psyche or mind as far as we know is housed in the brain. The brain is encapsulated in the skull. There are two hemispheres to the brain each with separate, distinct functions. Pleasure and pain areas have been isolated. The section of the brain that controls logical thinking and verbal behavior is separate and distinct from the section that controls nonverbal behavior. It is very possible that the unconscious with which we struggle in mental health intervention has its locus in the nonverbal section of the brain. Brain research should continue to yield important information on this complex phenomenon we call the psyche.

With our present level of knowledge we must concede that the psyche is not definable. We can feed it knowledge, ideas, thoughts. We have no way of knowing or controlling the processing or the outcomes. The novelist George Eliot is said to have written letters to her unconscious assigning it specific tasks. Bertrand Russell, after extensive study of a given subject, is said to have ordered his unconscious to work underground while he went on to other things. The psyche has been compared to an artichoke. Peel away one layer and another surfaces. There is a kaleidoscopic quality to it too. It responds to and reflects the varying circumstances to which it is subjected. A graphic example is found in the South African pygmies. Their behavior in their natural habitat, the forest, is markedly different from their behavior in the negro village. There are aspects of their life and culture to which only the natives are privy.

As one considers all of this, it seems that the medical model may well be not only inadequate, but inappropriate to mental health intervention. What we need in its stead is a Human Potentialities Model. Such a model would focus on the individual's highest capabilities. Inadequacies and maladaptations would be considered only as they interfere with the individual's self-fulfillment.

For the component parts of such a model, Abraham Maslow has suggested that we look to the characteristics of the most accomplished individuals. Gardner Murphy points out that potentials emerge and can be realized only in a social context.

Consequently if we were to develop a Human Potentialities Model we would need to give consideration to the kind of world we are likely to face, the kind of world with which people must be prepared to cope.

The Emerging World

PROJECTIONS
It is projected that by 1981 there will be a chemical that will stop the aging process and reverse it. The body will maintain itself at age 25, the age of cell maturation. The brain will continue to develop and function in its established pattern. Biologists believe there is in the human body the same mechanism that in the salamander restores body parts as they wear out or fail to function. They hope to locate this mechanism and to activate it. Current organ-replacement programs would be rendered unnecessary.

Rocket travel will make it possible for us to travel from New York to London in 20 minutes; from New York to Tokyo in 45. Knowledge which has expanded 100 times since 1900 will continue to develop in geometric progression. With the electronic equipment now available it will be possible for an individual of average intelligence to acquire a B.A. degree in 180 hours of TV cassette listening; and to learn as many as 40 languages in a lifetime.

Regarding economics, in 1947 Paul Goodman wrote a book, *Communitas*. In it he presented seven possible blueprints for society. One intrigued me especially and still does. In it he projected that an individual will need to work one year in seven or a total of six or seven years in a lifetime to earn his basic maintenance. If he wanted a custom-built house or a custom-built car he might have to work a bit more in society-assigned tasks. The rest of the time he could do as he pleased. The March 1976 issue of *Scientific American* reports that by 1980 Japan hopes to complete a model for an unmanned factory manufacturing machine parts. This model is expected to be the prototype for all industrial countries. Should this materalize, Paul Goodman's projection may well be just around the corner.

Long life without aging, extended leisure without economic

need, knowledge expanding at an unprecedented rate requires a new perception of the life experience; new personality equipment. I propose the development of a Human Potentialities Model with three clearly specified goals:

- Autonomy
- Authenticity
- Accountability

These three A's could be the new Prescription for Good Mental Health (AAA—The New Prescription for Good Mental Health). They could become the new guideline, the new standard for mental health intervention in an insurance-based, health-focused service system. What a challenging enterprise with which to usher in our twenty-first century.

Appendix

One finds in the literature reference to 20 personality theories, 13 theories related to the dynamics of change and 52 procedures but without specification. At the 1975 I-CAPP Conference I was asked to itemize the theories and procedures to which I had referred.

The following is my attempt to fulfill that request. It represents my gleanings from five sources: Rapaport, Sarason, Kiernan, Wolberg, [and] Ford and Urban.* Sarason makes clear that when one speaks of "theories of personality" one is using the word theory not in its precise, scientific sense. One is using it rather to designate theoretical orientations, hypotheses, formulations, interpretations. One finds also that most of the personality theories are identified by author and proponent rather than by concept.

The following [Table] deals only with "theories of personality," not "theories of therapy." The "Core Issue" relates to the factor or factors central to the particular theory and the determinant in therapeutic procedures. Under "Change Dynamic" I have listed the components considered most essential to the therapeutic process.

* See Notes.

Personality Theory	Core Issue	Change Dynamic
Freud	Sexuality and the Unconscious	Free Association
Adler	Superiority-Inferiority	Relationship with Therapist
Jung	Collective Unconscious	Exploration
Rank	Birth Trauma; The Will	Will-Counterwill
Theodore Reik	Psychic Dependency	Nurturance
Horney	The Self and Social Relationships	Exploration, Past and Present
Sullivan	Culture and Interpersonal	Elucidation
Carl Rogers	Self-Actualization	Empathy
Maslow	Self-Esteem	Value-Oriented Model
Erikson	Identity Crisis	Empathy-Sympathy
Wilhelm Reich	Defenses: The Character Armor	Interpretation
William James	Knowledge	Thought
Gestalt (Fritz Perls)	Total Personality Configuration	Awareness and Insight
Dynamic (Kurt Lewin; Gardner Murphy)	Perception of Reality	Differentiation-Integration
Existential (Rollo May)	Personality Authenticity	Understanding the Present
Ego Analysis (Hartmann, Holt, Rapaport)	Autonomy of the Ego	Awareness
Phenomenological (Sartre)	Organism-Environment Interaction	Content of Language
Humanistic (Allport)	Interests, Values, Principles	Self-awareness
Cybernetics	Psychophysiological Organism	Appeal to creativity and individual differences
Learning (Dollard and Miller)	Innate and Learned Drives	Reward, Reinforcement

There may be other and additional formulations that might qualify under the rubric of "Personality Theory" as it is here employed. An analysis of all of them for overlapping and mutually exclusive elements might well further the development of a unified personality theory so urgently needed in the understanding and development of mental health interventions.

PROCEDURES

Delineation of the 52 procedures has required search, selection and elaboration. What follows is open to question, modification, amplification. I invite your involvement.

Among the procedures involved in the therapeutic process are:

Exploration	Educate
Explication	Reeducate
Clarification	Anticipate
Interpretation	Rehearse
Extrapolation	Challenge
Accounting	Confrontation
Assessment	Detection
Generalization	Election
Cathexis	Correction
Synthesis	Conditioning
Discovery	Drive Reduction
Invention	Role Playing
Elaboration	Observation
Modification	Persuasion
Reinforcement	Sharing
Sorting	Stimulating
Selection	Intervening
Direction	Maintenance
Binding	Nurturance
Restraint	Externalization
Mediation	Internalization
Priming	Insight Development
Diffusion	Option Identity
Intellectualizing	Projection
Eroticizing	Manipulation
Desensitizing	Application

The experience I have had in trying to make specific the generalizations of the number of personality theories, change dynamics and procedures, demonstrates graphically that the entire field of psychotherapy has been remiss in defining the specifics of practice. It is a challenge that takes on urgency as prospects for an insurance-based service system develop.

Bibliography

American Hospital Association, *Analyses of National Health Insurance Proposals* (Chicago: American Hospital Association, 1974).

Bertalanffy, Ludwig von, *General System Theory* (New York: Braziller, 1968).

The Center Magazine, various issues.

Ford, Donald, and Urban, Hugh, *Systems of Psychotherapy* (New York: Wiley, 1965).

Gill, Merton M., ed., *The Collected Papers of David Rapaport* (New York: Basic Books, 1967).

Goodman, Paul and Percival, *Communitas* (New York: Vintage, 1960).

The Humanist, various issues.

Kiernan, Thomas, *Shrinks, etc.* (New York: Dial, 1974).

Pearce, Joseph, *The Crack in the Cosmic Egg* (New York: Julian Press, 1974).

Phillips, E. L., and Weiner, D. N., *Short-Term Psychotherapy and Structured Behavior Change* (New York: McGraw-Hill, 1966).

Psychology Today, various issues.

Sarason, Irwin G., *Personality: An Objective Approach* (New York: Wiley, 1972).

Saturday Review, various issues.

Scientific American, various issues.

Toffler, Alvin, *Future Shock* (New York: Random House, 1970).

Wolberg, Lewis, *The Technique of Psychotherapy* (New York: Grune & Stratton, 1954).

CHAPTER 4

Packaging for National Health Insurance: the Human Potential Model*

Preface

This presentation is the third step in a process initiated in I-CAPP at its fourteenth annual conference in Newport Beach, California (June 1975). Proposed at that conference was the proposition that I-CAPP commit itself to the development of a Human Potential Model to replace the traditional medical model in mental health intervention. The proposal achieved consensus. Implementation was recognized as a long-range task.

In June 1976 at the I-CAPP Conference in Toronto, Canada, participants accepted the challenge of constituting themselves, for the duration of the specific session, the equivalent of the Club Rome** in mental health intervention. With the paper: "Comprehensive National Health Insurance: What It May Mean to the Mental Health Practitioner" as the frame of reference, the group undertook to identify the characteristics that might go into a Human Potential Model,† considering what the world that is emerging may require.

* Presented at the 16th Annual I-CAPP Conference, San Antonio, Texas, June 26, 1977.

** A small group of experts from many countries and many fields who meet periodically to develop a blueprint for a global society.

† See Appendix.

"The greatest discovery of my generation," said William James, "is that human beings can alter their lives by altering their attitude of mind." The concept of human potential brings this "discovery" into focus and gives it centrality hopefully to serve as the foundation for life-sustaining, life-enhancing services to people whatever their intrinsic capacities, whatever their station in life.

Packaging the Human Potential Model in a way that it could be recognized as the very foundation of good health in its many, varied dimensions was seen by I-CAPP '76 as essential before seeking visibility and support for the issue. The following represents a beginning effort at such packaging. If it proves valid, feasible, practical, the question we will then need to address is what, how, when do we venture into the public arena to break ground in this evolutionary move which must be seen clearly as revolutionary in its potential impact.

A delay seems imminent as far as national health insurance is concerned. This gives added impetus, pertinence and perhaps even urgency to this effort. Thompson R. Fulton put it so well in his presentation to the Social Welfare Forum [1976], we should be interested in "not just some kind of National Health Insurance" but in the kind that will serve people best in the future that lies ahead.

Introduction

Richard Grossman asserts: "There is no such thing as physical health or mental health or psychological health or emotional health. None of these can be separated from the wholeness of the person. Health is the actualization of all that is latent and potential in us. We are at any given moment healthy to the degree that we are manifesting our possibilities . . . our wholeness." A person may be handicapped by a withered hand but this does not stop him from using the rest of what he has to the fullest. Grossman reminds us that we have our bodies. The body is our connection with the world. But we are "not our bodies." [1]

There has been a preoccupation with our bodies that some view as a virtual obsession. There has been a delegation of power and influence to the physician commensurate with the "obsession." The larger whole, the human being, seems to have been lost along the way. Certainly not with intent. Rather, the human mind unable to comprehend the total in its complexity has partialized the task and quite appropriately undertaken to master the simpler aspect. The body is visible. It is tangible. It lends itself to weight, measurement, instrumental, electrical, chemical intrusion. It has an observable growth-decline developmental sequence.

The mind—the thinking, feeling, observing, reasoning—aspect of the human personality is illusive. It reaches all parts of the body. It serves to adjust the total organism to the needs and demands of the environment. It is not visible. It is not tangible. The mind has a developmental sequence; but it is a sequence that does not lend itself easily to standardization. The development of the mind can be delayed, blocked, restricted, constricted, distorted by life experiences, real or imagined. There is no quick and easy way to ascertain whether a three- to six-year-old is mastering the task of sexual identity or the family romance. Similarly there is no simple, easy way of determining to what extent unresolved archaic fantasies and erroneous perceptions are playing a part in adult conflict, maladjustment, frustration.

It would be unfair not to acknowledge the tremendous achievements in understanding the operation of our physical structure, in disease control, in organ replacement. Current efforts to control or possibly stop the aging process, to procreate without mating, to duplicate individuals via cloning are impressive and if successful may precipitate radical change in world population and world management.

These very achievements, striking as they are, cast in bold relief the lacks that have persisted. It has been known for many years that certain physical disorders are strongly influenced if not induced by certain emotional states. Best known among these are asthma, colitis, the allergies. One finds occasionally in the literature the suggestion that there might be an emotional component in cancer. Recently there was reported research findings to the effect that persons suffering coronary disease were found to be experiencing dissatisfactions, on jobs, in their environment; that they had experienced long-term frustrations, stress and losses. The research revealed also that certain personality characteristics were present among those suffering coronary artery disease: excessive drive for advancement and achievement; competitiveness; many involvements; difficulty with authority; exterior calm coupled with aggressive impulses; well-established patterns of denial and repression.[2] In the light of this awareness of long standing it is amazing that the medical profession has done little, if anything to get to the roots of stress-related illnesses.

An equally amazing phenomenon exists in our current handling of suicide. Suicide is fast approaching an international epidemic. Except where public figures are concerned suicide is a nonfact. In all mass media it is dealt with as "death"; not as "murder," the murder of self. This is a considered, deliberate approach, not by accident. It is based on the theory that acknowledgment will give impetus to the self-destructive impulse. If epidemics of measles, smallpox, polio, tuberculosis had been handled with this ostrich technique one might well wonder what the state of these illnesses would be today. Who is standing in the way of a full psychosocial autopsy on every suicide? Are we afraid to explore the antecedents to the murderous act? Are we afraid to consider the influences that induce vulnerability, incite acting out? Perhaps some of the psychic interventions intended to promote health are for some people the "last straw," life destroying. Perhaps there are psychic procedures of an antiseptic nature that would be protective, preventive. Certainly the ostrich approach is invalid, inappropriate, and thoroughly irresponsible.

Also, suicide itself has many dimensions. The final and irreversible state of physical death is only one. There is psychological suicide in depression, in the psychoses, drugs, alcohol. There is social suicide in isolation, withdrawal, inertia, apathy, hostility, aggression. Again the psychological dimension of human experience takes on a pervasiveness, a centrality outweighing by far in scope and effect that of the human body.

The Human Potential Concept

The human potential concept rooted in a theory of human growth and development and committed to the goal of the "pursuit of happiness" as a constitutional human right might lead to many changes, among them, changes in terminology. Instead of Comprehensive Community Mental Health Centers we might have Comprehensive Human Enhancement Services. Instead of Comprehensive National Health Insurance we might have Comprehensive National Human Resource Insurance with compensation for resources that are underdeveloped, underused, exploited, depleted, damaged. We might have Comprehensive National Human Enrichment Insurance protecting the right of each individual to appropriate, quality education, training, acculturation and of course necessary nutrition, protection (physical, psychological, social) and medical care.

In other words, viewing the human estate in terms of potential rather than pathology may provide new vistas, new perspectives, new insights, new instruments for the enhancement of the individual and for the enhancement of the human life experience.

This change in view is no simple task. Furthermore, the implications and the ramifications are monumental. As a society we will undertake the task only if we are convinced that we have no choice. Indicators that we are fast approaching that stage abound in the number of people who resort to alcohol, tranquilizers, drugs, in the ever-growing number of young, educated, talented people who commit suicide; and in the high proportion (estimated as at least two-thirds) of people frequenting medical facilities who are ill but in whom there is no discernible pathology; and in the high incidence of depression. Our society, affluent, accomplished, rich in variety apparently is failing somehow, somewhere in meeting the basic needs of the human being. Basic needs are still needs to be determined. Dr. Jonas Salk, of polio fame is said to be devoting full time to basic research in this area. In the meantime we may have to content ourselves with Dr. James Plant's observation, i.e., we learn from people with problems what aspects of life, living, relationships pose problems for everyone. Or we might look to our files where we probably have in massive detail clues to basic human needs. All that might be necessary would be an integrator or an integrating instrument to provide a total view of human life experiences and cause-effect relationships as basic human needs come into juxtaposition with societal needs, expectations, demands. The Human Potential Model conceivably could be such an integrating mechanism.

New Realities

According to Alvin Toffler, we are experiencing the second catastrophic change in human history, equivalent to the shift from primitive to civilized society.[3] By 1980, Japan expects to complete the model for an unmanned factory. By 1981, biochemists expect to perfect a chemical that will stop the aging process and reverse it. The body will remain at age 25 (cells being automatically replaced as they reach maturity). The brain will continue to develop without interruption. Biologists are hoping to locate in the human body the organ-replacement mechanism (similar to that in the salamander) which they believe has been rendered inactive during the process of evolution. Once located and reactivated, this mechanism would replace organs as they wear out or malfunction. Longevity estimates range from 800 years in five to ten years to immortality by 2091.[4]

There is evidence in more and more areas—banking, purchasing, communications, travel, medicine that automation will take over all routine tasks and specialized activities. The Maryland State Department of Education has received a federal grant of $427,000 to establish three "direction centers" to help match people with special educational needs and public and private services that might meet those needs. The centers are to be completely computerized. Diagnosis will be a part of the service and also a three-month follow-up to determine whether the plan that was put into effect was appropriate.[5] A machine is on the drawing boards that would yield a psychological diagnosis in 5 to 10 minutes that would normally take three to four days.

The global society is a reality. Instant intercontinental communication is a reality. With our present level of technology we could probably already rocket from New York to London in 20 minutes and to Tokyo in 45.

What is occurring slowly but surely, bit by bit, is a shift from man's being in the service of society to society's being in the service of man. This requires a major change in the perception of both man and society. Man will have to be viewed in terms of his needs and his capabilities. Society will have to viewed in terms of how well it is meeting man's needs; how well it is developing and utilizing man's capabilities. The move from a society-focused society to a people-focused society may be mandatory not elective; an essential not a frill; a matter of survival not a luxury. If the human being's needs are not met; if his capabilities are not provided development and expression, disorders result. The human being does not take well to frustration. Society becomes the victim, the loser on two scores. Society is deprived of the best of people capability. It must develop and pay for services to deal with the disorders resulting from unmet needs and frustrated capacity.

There is a timeliness to the proposed move from pathology to potential in planning services for the human life experience. Our world is in the throes of change on all levels. We are becoming more knowledgeable about the brain, the mind, the personality.

With the investigations now in progress we may soon know for instance whether: the brain operates on a source of energy separate from the body; whether specific functions—cognition, memory, feeling, etc., have a specific locus in the brain or are generalized processes. We may soon know how or if energy flow in the brain is affected by such human experiences as anger, hate, fear, anxiety, guilt, remorse. We soon may be able to determine if and how energy flow in the brain affects (excites, inhibits, blocks) such brain functions as cognition, memory, affect. We may soon be able to determine whether certain emotional experiences affect energy flow in the brain affecting differentially specific brain functions. In other words, the brain is well on the way to becoming as well charted as the body. We may anticipate that as our knowledge is expanded so will be the variety of interventions. Mental health intervention as we know it today may be only one of many varieties in the human life services system of the future.

New Perspectives

Our federal government insures corporations against loss of their businesses through government takeover in foreign countries. In 1970 a 73-year-old attorney in California filed suit against the government for a depletion allowance for himself and his 69-year-old wife, their bodies, their skills, similar to what is allowed in industry for mineral depletion. After a three-year battle the court ruled against him. Why shouldn't individuals be insured against loss of self-esteem, self-gratification, self-fulfillment through tasks that are unchallenging, marriages that are unsuccessful, education that is inadequate or inappropriate, life experiences that interfere with personal development, relationships, learning, functioning; the hazards of arrested intellectual and emotional growth. Perhaps there should be tax rebates or bonuses for marriages of long standing, for children who perform maximally in school, for people who perform maximally in their jobs, in marriage in child-rearing. We might begin to think in terms of:

- A Human Resources Index: Intelligence, Aptitudes, Talents, Interests
- A Human Potential Realization Audit
- A Gross National Product Audit of Human Potentials

The Census which is taken every 10 years could easily be expanded to include questions of interests, aptitudes, talents, realized, unrealized, etc., for a beginning estimate of service needs and service areas if we are to be committed to the goals of "life, liberty and the pursuit of happiness."

Old Truths Reviewed and Reaffirmed

Essential to human well-being is the sense of meaning and direction, the sense of self and of self-worth; conviction that life is worthwhile and a privilege; a commitment to the highest of human social values; honesty, justice, integrity, trust.

Essential to the human potential view is the realization that the human being is intrinsically in embryo, in an undeveloped stage as long as he lives. There is no age limit to continued development. (To what extent this is true for those individuals who have suffered severe psychological impairment remains to be explored.) Development requires awareness of possibilities, of opportunities, of options, of investment and risks. Development requires anticipation, hope, faith, confidence in one's strength, confidence in one's judgment, confidence in one's capacity to survive failure, disappointment, hurt.

We need to be reminded that behavior does not change by edict, on demand. Behavior changes as one's perceptions change; as one's knowledge is expanded or corrected; as one's feelings about oneself become more appropriate. We must remember that self-discovery and self-realization are undertakings that take a lifetime. The human being is genetically equipped with many intricate faculties. He can experience the present, remember the past, anticipate the future. He can experience and respond to multiple stimuli reaching him at the same time. He is capable of in-depth and subliminal perception, monitoring, processing, registering, reacting. He has tremendous strength. He is very fragile. His strengths and his frailties are important indicators in the assessment of potential, as are the sources from which his strengths and weaknesses stem.

Just as the human being's faculties are many and varied, so are his needs. His needs in fact are often contradictory. He wants security at the same time he yearns for variety and excitement. He longs for roots and dreams of wings. He wants to be surrounded by the familiar and protests the lack of challenge. We are learning how susceptible the human being is to outside influence. A recent experiment demonstrated that one can induce aging in 18- to 24-year-olds through attitude and expectations. Conversely, perhaps we can induce youthfulness through attitude and expectations where older individuals are concerned. Voodoo in primitive societes seems to have capitalized on this human phenomenon. Wish a person dead, tell him he will die; and he accommodates.

Among our perceptions of people there are some that are based on wishful thinking, on erroneous assumptions that persist in spite of knowledge to the contrary and experience. We approach the neglecting parent as though his neglect is subject to conscious, rational control. We view the nonlearning student as defiant, obstinate, amenable to suggestion, direction, punishment. How simple the task of social workers and educators would be were these assumptions valid. How difficult the task becomes when one considers that the parent's neglect may be due to inadequate or erroneous perception of reality rooted in his preoccupation with fantasy. How complex the task of the educator when he addresses himself to the possibility that the nonlearning student is anxiety-ridden due to unresolved, archaic worries, fears, guilts.

In each of these instances, anger, impatience, admonition are to no avail. Assessment of capabilities is essential: capabilities that are operational, capabilities which can be expanded through education, suggestion, therapy; capabilities that are inadequate to the situation in which the individual finds himself and for which there must be supplementation from the outside or substitution.

Applying industrial concepts to the human estate and equipped with a blueprint of the brain, we may find ourselves thinking in terms of energy—energy reserves, depletion, misdirection. We may find ourselves thinking in terms of moratorium, borrowing, substitution, supplementation, replacement. We may see adolescent depression as the search for a new equilibrium; cyclical disorders as reflecting oscillations in psychic energy. We may give more thought to how psychic energy can be replenished, reinforced, expanded. For instance, travel, a change of routine, a new activity might be an energy source and as such viewed as a necessity not a luxury or indulgence.

A Human Potential Accounting System: or An H.R.S. (Human Resource Survey)

The industrial frame of reference may provide us also with a new accounting system. The human being as a resource elicits a very different response, very different perceptions than the human being as responsibility, a burden, a necessary evil. With the goal that of maximizing the resource the approach to need takes on a distinctly different focus.

Since the human estate is multidimensional, the accounting system must have scope and definitiveness. It must include: Genetic Equipment; Developmental Achievements, Deficiences, Impairments; Perceptions; Goals; Lifestyle, Physical Health, etc. The accounting system would need two major categories: (1) Inventory and Assessment, and (2) Intervention: Target and Technique.

With the total spectrum of the individual's situation in view and in computerizable form, the computer could become a most effective instrument for pinpointing the issues central to the individual's concern and for selecting target and technique for intervention.

The following [Charts, pages 80–82,] are a pioneer effort at formulating a Human Potential Accounting System. Your considered appraisal and suggestions are invited.

Differences of opinion between the applicant and the practitioner could easily be noted. Survey findings could lend themselves to computerization and thence to cross-referencing and correlation. Clues to the possible effect of situational, social, psychological stress upon physical well-being might be readily ascertainable. Selection of the most effective, efficient, economical interventions might be facilitated as well as periodic review and assessment of outcomes.

On May 10, 1977 the Cleveland *Plain Dealer* reported a 25 percent increase in the number of hysterectomies performed between 1970 and 1975; a total of 725,000 according to the National Health Center for Health Statistics. Doctors at a House Subcommittee meeting in Washington the day before had acknowledged that surgical intervention is sometimes undertaken to relieve anxiety. What an indictment of the health professions. Are we indeed like the six blind men and the elephant, each convinced that the part he perceives is the whole? The findings of the committee which for two years studied unneeded surgery present cogent data to support the proposal that we need, urgently, a comprehensive view of the human being in planning all interventive procedures.

Human Potential Accounting System
Part I: Personal Attributes: Inventory and Assessment
(High, Moderate, Low, Uncertain, Unknown)
ATTRIBUTES

Genetic Equipment
Intelligence
Physical Health
Physical Appearance
Motor equipment

Developmental Achievements
Autonomy
Authenticity
Accountability

Personality Characteristics
Curiosity
Enthusiasm
Courage
Resourcefulness
Persistent
Flexible
Dependable
Good Judgment

Developmental Deficits
Narcissism
Self-Other fusion (symbiosis)
Dependency
Ego-diffusion (indeterminate sense of self)
Archaic perceptions (infantilism)
Archaic expectations:
  of self
  of others
  of situations

Impairments
Education vis-à-vis potential and
  desire
Social Situation
  Broken Home (parents')
  Broken Home (own)
  Isolation—by choice
  Isolation—imposed

Employment
  Underplaced
  Overplaced
  Underemployed
  Overemployed
  Interested
  Disinterested
  Challenged
  Bored

Perceptions
Self:
  Accurate
  Inaccurate
  Overassessed
  Underassessed
Others:
  Accurate
  Inaccurate
  Overassessed
  Underassessed
Life:
  Optimistic
  Pessimistic
  Indifferent
  Apathetic
  Uninvolved
  Protesting
  Defensive
  Resistent
  Energetic
  Imaginative

Human Potential Accounting System
Part II: Social Situation: Inventory and Assessment
Social Situation

Opportunities
Economic
Educational
Social
Recreational
Spatial
Other (specify)

Activities
Economic
Educational
Social
Recreational
Spatial
Other (specify)

Relationships
Parents
Siblings
Relatives
Spouse
Children
Other (specify)

Part III: Interferences to Realization of Potential: External; Internal

External
Economics
Education
Social Situation:
  Marriage
  Parenthood
  Other (specify)

Internal

Physical Equipment
  superior
  adequate
  poor
    impaired: temporary
          permanent

Energy Level:
  superior
  adequate
  poor:
    impaired
    obstructed
    misdirected
    depleted
    suppressed

Psychological Equipment
  superior
  adequate
  poor:
    immature
    inhibited
    constricted:
      lack of knowledge
      lack of interest
      lack of motivation
    phobic
    anxious
    guilt-ridden
    archaic perceptions
    inertia
    apathy
    inadequate goals

Specific Problems:
  alcohol
  drugs
  crime
  accident-proneness
  homicidal
  suicidal
  delusional
  depressed

Human Potential Accounting System
Part IV: Interventions: Sought (applicant);
Recommended (practitioner)

	Sought	Recommended
Economic		
Environment		
housing		
management		
child care		
other (specify)		
Social Status		
marriage		
separation		
divorce		
lifestyle (specify)		
Physical		
Diagnosis:		
discomfort		
disability		
other (specify)		
Treatment:		
nutritional		
chemical		
surgical		
other (specify)		
Psychological		
Diagnosis:		
discomfort		
disability		
Treatment:		
chemical		
behavioral		
intrapsychic		
psychiatrist		
psychologist		
social worker		
other (specify)		

Appendix

35 * personality characteristics found in persons of high achievement (and possibly relevant to the human potential concept in human services) are:

Self-Perception

unique
evolving
striving
autonomous
authentic
high self-esteem

Self-Representation

energetic
optimistic
adventuresome
forthright
expressive

Self-Experiencing

self-reliant
open
spontaneous
vigorous
curious
enterprising
trusting
motivated
sharing
receptive
sense of well-being

Other-Perception

separateness
acceptance of difference
  as enriching
trust, respect

Other-Involvement

understanding
empathetic
reciprocal
caring
sharing
problem solving, not
  conflict
open

Notes

1. Grossman, Richard, "The Whole Picture of Health," *Quest '77* (January/February 1977), vol. 1, no. 1 (Pasadena, Calif.: Ambassador International Cultural Foundation).
2. Sokol, Bernice, "The Clinical Social Worker as a Member of a Health Team in a Coronary Care Unit," *Clinical Social Work Journal* (Winter 1976), vol. 4, no. 4.
3. Toffler, Alvin, *Future Shock* (New York: Random House, 1971).
4. Bjorksten, Johan, and Martin, Rolf, in "Unhooked," The Cleveland *Plain Dealer*, September 3, 1976.
5. *Human Sciences Feature* (Spring 1977).

* "openness" appeared in three categories; "sharing" in two; and "trusting" in two. A net total of 31 characteristics have been identified.

Bibliography

The Humanist, various issues.
Murphy, Gardner, *Human Potentialities* (New York: Basic Books, 1958).
NIH Research Advances, 1976.
Psychology Today, various issues.
Saturday Review, various issues.
Scientific American, various issues.

CHAPTER 5

Basic Needs and Social Survival*

Introduction

This discussion of basic needs is limited. It concerns itself with the psychological dimension of the human personality, not for all time but for this point in time. Essential to the thesis is the view that the human being is in the continuous process of evolution. His genetic equipment is embryonic at birth. It is subject to development in depth, breadth and scope not yet fully recognized or appreciated even by the most adventuresome minds. The proposition that the human brain consists of 15 billion brain cells only half of which have been activated, and that the most accomplished human beings use only 5 to 10 percent of the activated brain cells poses possibilities literally beyond comprehension.

Psychologists claim to have identified 70 different intelligences and estimate there may be 50 more. This we can begin to consider using as a starting point the five senses and their component parts. Hypothesizing that each "intelligence" might have its own distinctive boundaries and developmental sequence, the prospect of human potential takes on added dimension.

Given the human being in the process of evolution, acculturated to meet the needs of an industrial society, what is the task that faces us as we find ourselves catapulted into the post-

* Presented at the 17th Annual I-CAPP Conference, Charleston, S.C. June 1978.

industrial world? The projected postindustrial world is likely to be characterized by:

- long life without aging; organs automatically replaced as in the salamander once they become malfunctioning
- extended leisure without economic need; the prospect that retirement will begin with birth
- home-centered education via satellite
- rocket travel making it possible to span continents in less time than it takes from a central city to the airport
- international conferences via telecommunication

The postindustrial world is likely to be "one" world not for humanitarian reasons but for sheer survival of the human species. World order that has eluded the talents of diplomats may emerge an unexpected dividend of international industry. In the interest of profit may be accomplished what has not been attainable in the interest of human welfare. An interesting phenomenon should it occur. A travesty on the intrinsic nature of man? Perhaps. Equally possible, however, is it that man at his current stage of psychological development has not been capable of the higher motive. This does not put past or beyond man the possibility that in the next stage of his psychological development the higher level motives may prevail. This remains to be seen.

World order presupposes world peace. With world peace guaranteed it will be possible for us to redirect, refocus our attention and energies from survival to the further development of man, to enrich life experience, toward the fulfillment of human potential. Where do we start as we contemplate where we would like to go from where we are?

A Pristine Look

We need first of all to look at the human being afresh, as though we have never seen him before. We need to consider what psychological equipment the human being has; what experiences, impressions, expectation he brings with him as he emerges forcefully or benignly from the womb. We need to consider how our processes of nurturing, acculturating, educating affect the equipment, the impressions, the expectations with which he comes into the world of people, things, and events.

Marshall McLuhan suggests that the central nervous system of the human species may be experiencing life-threatening implosion by the modern inventions of printing, the radio, and TV taxing the cognitive, the auditory and the visual equipment with which the species is endowed. Numbness and apathy are the living system's response to such intrusion. Anxiety with which electronic developments were greeted at the beginning has been replaced by boredom,[1] a withdrawal from the challenge that could be represented in the development of the "global village," the product of jet travel, and satellite communication. "The effects of technology," says McLuhan, "do not occur at the level of opinions and concepts, but alter patterns of perception. . . ." It is possible he postulated that traditions which were eroded during the industrialized period will have to be rediscovered and developed for the human being to be able to cope with the demands of the electronic age. Hope as he sees it rests in the increase in human autonomy, in the ability to anticipate what may lie ahead.[2]

Indicators that the human species may be experiencing "life-threatening implosion" as McLuhan suggests are many. Americans consume 27 million pounds of aspirin in one year; 70 million people drink alcohol; 19 million suffer chronic depression. One and one-half million individuals are admitted to mental hospitals in a year. Suicides are the third cause of death among young children; second among students and successful graduates of advanced education. (Among teenagers, the number of suicides has tripled since the 1950s.) Those figures take on a sobering significance when we are reminded as we are by Loren Eiseley that 90 percent of the world's species have perished.[3] We may be an endangered species.

Added to the statistics is the pervasive lament among people of all walks of life about aloneness, loneliness, isolation, the feeling of emptiness, rootlessness. What is there about the current life circumstance that creates the feeling of desolation; the feeling of abandonment? At the root of our problems may well be the breakup of the extended family. In the extended family one had virtually guaranteed safety, belongingness, significance. Traditionally where family is concerned as Robert Frost puts it: "They have to take you in." One does not have to be liked or loved. One is assured that one will be guaranteed a place. That is the world that was. Today the so-called "family" may find itself in a mobile home, in a one-room efficiency condominium; on the East Coast in the summer, on the West Coast in winter. The "welcome mat" may still exist psychologically but not spatially. And one's unrootedness, one's uprootedness is dramatized. The annual pilgrimage home may be mass denial of an objective reality; that "home" and family exist primarily in fantasy; that one is on one's own. One is alone.

It is possible, says Jacques Cousteau, that the industrial revolution has created a sudden discontinuity in the human "ecosystem," in man's essential patterns of interdependency. New patterns may need to be developed. In the meantime transient or intermediate arrangements may be necessary.

Ecology, which is the study of the interrelationship of organisms with each other, may provide some clues to the nature of the dislocations man seems to be experiencing at the present time. Marine biology may provide some significant insights to the variety of adaptations we observe in human society. Aquatic organisms and the human organism have one thing in common: each inhabits an ocean. Fish inhabit an ocean of water. Man inhabits an ocean of air. We know that oceans of water are affected by "wind, the rotation of the earth, the gravitational pull of the sun and moon, the differing densities of warm and cold water." [4] We do not know yet what currents of nature affect the human being. In recent years only the very barest of beginnings has been made in this by the environmentalists. A "new world" remains to be discovered and explored. Survival of the human species is the focal point; the core issue.

Marine life and human life have in common a space delimited environment, each with specific, unique characteristics. Is it possible they have in common patterns of adaptation that relate to the commonality of "being alive" rather than to species specificity? Marine biologists have found for instance that fish travel in schools until adulthood and then they lead a more solitary existence. Is it possible that in the human species too there may be a period when "people need people", and that there might be periods when the individual needs to be alone?

Marine biologists also find different patterns of interdependency in the aquatic community. There is "symbiosis" where two dissimilar organisms live together or exchange services for the benefit of both. There is "communalism" where two organisms live together: one benefits, the other is unaffected; or one benefits to the detriment of the other (parasitism). There is the kind of communalism where one is attached to another; or takes shelter in another. There is the kind of communalism where each benefits mutually. In reference to the phenomenon of schooling marine biologists ask such questions as: how does schooling promote the survival of the species? They have found that it protects the species from predators; promotes learning; promotes group memory. They found that schooling occurs at breeding time, feeding time, sometimes at random and at times of stress.

As we take a fresh, pristine look at the human being perhaps we need to ask similar questions and be alert to similar variations.

The Promise of the Womb: A Hoax

Otto Rank in his book *The Trauma of Birth*,[5] written in 1924, asserted that the human being never recovers from the trauma of birth. He considered this experience central to personality development. It was on this issue that he and Freud parted professional company. Freud considered sexuality central to personality development. Interestingly, our society "bought" Freud's concept of the centrality of sex. In fact, our society has made of sex the sin qua non of everything. If you are good in sex you are good in everything: you are likable, lovable, bright, competent and all the other positive attributes we value. If you don't "make" it sexually you might as well "throw in the sponge" in the arena of life. What a misrepresentation of facts. If you are good in sex, you are good in sex. Sex does not generalize.

Be that as it may. While our society has made of sex the symbol of all that is good, beautiful and worthwhile, it has virtually ignored in its consideration of human needs the in-womb experience, what part it has played in the evolution of human personality: in the equipment the human psyche brings to the life experience, the expectations that the human psyche may have derived from it and the kind of nurturing, socialization and indoctrination the psyche might need to equip it to deal with the objective realities of life in the society in which it finds itself.

As one thinks about it, the human being from the instant of conception, has experienced automatic satisfaction of his needs at every stage of intrauterine experience. Needs and wants were met probably without conscious awareness that there were needs or wants. (We do not know yet what level of conscious awareness exists in the embryo at the many stages of intrauterine development. This may become clear as sophisticated electronic instruments for investigation become available.)

Evidence that the in-womb experience leaves a lasting mark on the human psyche abounds. We go through life believing that just "being" is enough. The fact that we "are" entitles us to love. If we are not loved totally, completely, without reservation as we fantasize we should be, we conclude that there must be something intrinsically wrong with us. We go through life expecting that those who "love" us know without our telling them what we like, what we think, what we feel. If they do not, our confidence in how they feel about us is shaken. We engage in the eternal search for the one-and-only, the "forever" relationship that will be available under any and all circumstances as our needs require.

The search for the one-and-only, "forever," fused relationship (two-makes-one) is a futile one. Only once in a lifetime does such a relationship exist—in the womb. Once we are born, once we are equipped with the essentials for separate existence, for independent survival we are ejected from the base that spawned and nurtured our being. We find ourselves in a totally foreign environment that calls into play as never before the physical, psychological, social armamentarium that constitutes the human estate.

Preparation for the Out-of-Womb Experience— The Real World

Nothing in the intrauterine experience has prepared the psyche for the out-of-womb experience. It is not likely that the psyche in-embryo has had any inkling of what would be entailed in the world beyond the womb. In-embryo the psyche has known at-oneness with another; movement cushioned by embryonic fluid, sounds varied in content and intensity, and only the very faintest of light. Ejection from the womb must also come without preparation, except perhaps the preparation that might come from being in an enclosure less and less adequate for survival.

The birth process, unless it is surgical, is inevitably stressful. The stress may be of short or long duration. Psychological researchers in recent years have discovered that traumatic experiences of short duration leave no permanent imprint on the psyche. If this is true, individuals whose birth occurred quickly or surgically may have no permanent birth imprint related to the birth experience itself. This would not be true for the in-womb experience. Nine months in the womb must have left a deep, indelible impression on the psyche. The experience and the psychological effects of it are an absolute in human experience. It is universal. Yet little if any attention has been given to it.

We know well the physical umbilical cord. It is carefully severed at birth and permitted to self-destruct. Few theorists have ventured the possibility that there might be a psychological umbilical cord as well. Since we have not even acknowledged the possibility of its existence we certainly have given no attention to how the psychological umbilical cord if it exists can be severed or rendered inoperative.

As we observe people in their eternal search for a replica of the womb we might consider that the psychological umbilical cord may be the culprit. It is possible that never having been severed or rendered inoperative it may continue to function through life. It may continue to hold for the individual the promise that the womb still exists; that if we persist long enough, are worthy enough we will find it and it will be ours forever.

Social indoctrination confirming this fantasy begins early. Only recently on the TV program "ZOOM," a children's program written and performed by children for children, had as its theme song: "I need you to need me and you need it too." Other popular songs keep alive the fantasy and sell people a "bill of goods" that is just not accurate or valid. The song Barbra Streisand made popular: "People who need people are the luckiest people on earth" is one example. Another is: "You're nobody until somebody loves you." Actually it isn't likely anyone will love you until you are "somebody." Psychological hoaxes can be perpetrated by song writers out of their misperceptions or to suit the purposes of a particular enterprise like the theme of a story. The fact that these hoaxes gain popularity indicates that they fit the psychological needs, the perceptions of the populace.

Furthermore, the psyche is inventive. It indulges in many psychological disguises; many artifices, many denials. Lifestyles, social institutions can provide structures that delude the psyche into a sense of security similar to what it experienced in the womb. When these arrangements end naturally as in the instance of graduation from school, or retirement from a job, or with death in a marriage; when they end unnaturally as through divorce or unemployment, the psyche suffers panic. It can suffer disorientation. It can suffer unsettling distress. All of this with an intensity not logical to the reality; to logical, rational understanding. The reaction, extreme as it is must come from the unconscious, from arational sources and might well be similar to what the psyche suffered at the time of physical birth.

To help the psyche master the new reality with which it is faced we must make clear from the moment of birth and repeat over and over again in whatever form is comprehensible to the individual at each and every stage of his development these undeniable, unmodifiable, absolute realities:

Once born there is no womb or equivalent thereof to which one can return.

Aloneness is intrinsic to the human estate.

Once out of the womb, just "being" is not enough for having all one's needs and wants satisfied. One must make one's needs and wants known. (How shocked the 21-year-old was when I asked her what made her lovable. It had never occurred to her that anything more than just "being" was necessary. What an injustice her nurturers and socializers had done to her.)

Maxwell Maltz explains: "A human being always acts and feels and performs in accordance with what he imagines to be true about himself and his environment. This is a basic law of the mind. It is the way we are built." [6] This taken together with Kenneth Boulding's assertion: "If the human race is to survive . . . it will have to change more in its ways of thinking in the next twenty-five years than it has done in the last 25,000 years," [7] poses a challenge of momentous proportions to those involved in nurturing, acculturation and education.

Acculturation

In the light of the in-womb experience and the out-of-womb reality, there are three absolutes that should form the foundation, the undergirding of all nurturing, acculturational and educational processes: *Aloneness*, *Separateness* and *Otherness*. These are the irreversibles, the unalterables, the constants of the human estate.

Aloneness is unconditional. Even if one has been part of multiple birth, one has been born singly, by oneself.

Companion to Aloneness and implicit in it is another absolute: Separateness: one is distinct. One is apart from all others. Companion to Separateness is Otherness. Just as one is distinct and apart from others so others are apart and distinct from one's self. This is so self-evident. Yet it is virtually impossible to accept; impossible to accommodate. The plea for "togetherness" is a longing for "oneness" with another, fusion—the two-makes-one fantasy. Our society supports and encourages the fantasy and the search. In fact it generates and promotes the view that aloneness is unfortunate, even disastrous, a signal of inadequacy.

Little wonder that in our mobile world without the buttressing of the family the human species is suffering such distress, such disorientation that survival may be in jeopardy. Saturday night is the loneliest night of the week; New Year's Eve is the loneliest night of the year. The socially isolated are 2 to 4 times as vulnerable as others to illness of the heart, digestion, respiratory system, accidents, suicide, even cancer.[8]

As of April 1978 there were 16 million individuals living alone in the U.S. Eight and one-tenth million men and women had been divorced and did not remarry. Of the divorced who did remarry 40 percent divorced a second time. Divorce increased 79 percent from 1970 to 1978. According to the U.S. Census report of March 1977 the number of unrelated men and women who lived together increased from 327,000 in 1970 to 754,000 in April 1978.[9] There seems to be little question that something is happening to the social institution known as "marriage." Something seems to be happening, too, to the man-woman relationship; perhaps even to relationships in general.

Relationships

It was the Romantics of the eighteenth century who promoted the concept of marriage as a union based on mutual love, (1) a composite of the physical and the spiritual (companionship), (2) equality of the partners, and (3) deemphasizing sexual differences. Interestingly, this concept developed in France and Germany. Neither of those countries "bought" it. It was exported to Britain and the United States. In the United States particularly the concept of romantic love was embraced without qualification and has been the accepted basis for marriage ever since.

At the very same time that the concept of romantic love was conceived and promoted, the Industrial Revolution was getting off the ground with urbanization, mobility and attendant weakening of family ties. Is it possible that "romantic love" emerged and flourished as an adaptation to the changes being brought about by the changes in society that rendered unavailable or unduly cumbersome the traditional mate-selection procedures, via family, kinship group, clan? Is it possible that in the centrality given sex in romantic love the psyche created the illusion of another womb—the fusion of two?

The current state of affairs—one of three marriages ending

in divorce—suggests that romantic love may not be a viable, tenable basis for an ongoing, in-depth relationship such as marriage is supposed to be. New adaptations to the processes of mate selection are developing. There is the computer dating service. Marriage brokers advertise their services in neighborhood newspapers. There are singles' groups that meet regularly. There are singles' bars. There are group tours for singles only. Some of the singles' enterprises specify age range. Some are interest focused; some are fun focused. Divested of the blood-related system of association, people devise new forms to meet unmet needs.

In the city of Cleveland, it is estimated that there are at least 200 singles' groups that meet at regular intervals. Options, therefore, are multiple. Selection becomes a problem. It requires a sorting out: a sorting out of who one is; what one wants to do with one's life; with whom does one want to share one's life experiences? Criteria for selection are complex. What should one look for in another person? How can one check the individual's authenticity; his accountability? How can one determine compatibility, and growth potential? With each individual left virtually to his own resources in mate selection it is important that individuals be informed, even trained so that they know what behavior means and what it portends for future development. An alternative or an addendum to this might be the requirement of premarital counseling much as one is required to have a blood test before marriage. Such a prerequisite would be feasible only if we became convinced that broken marriages involved serious risk to life. It would become feasible only if we had confidence that counseling would have an effect similar to that of innoculations against polio, smallpox, etc. We are a long way from either concern about the risk; a long way from confidence in the effectiveness of counseling as an immunization procedure.

In relationships other than marriage, criteria for selection are important also. If one has achieved autonomy—wholeness, self-sufficiency—relationships hold a special niche. They are the "frosting on the cake"; they are the whipped cream and maraschino cherry on the ice cream sundae. They are not sum and substance. They are frill. They are enrichment. They help in the dreaming of dreams. They help in making dreams come true. Relationships

of this character and quality are possible only if they are a "want"—
something desired; not if they are a "need"—something one
cannot do without. Relationships of this character and quality can
involve caring in-depth without comfort, security, belongingness.
If comfort, security, belongingness are present, fine. They are not
intrinsic to the situation. They are the pluses to the plus.

"It is only when we realize each other fully," say the O'Neills,[10]
"that we grow to the heights possible in man." Norman Cousins
on the same issue asserts: "We are largely illiterate in the knowledge of human relations." And a Case Western Reserve professor
asserted: "Man has learned to fly like a bird and swim like a fish
but not to live like a man." Our society abounds in evidence in
support of these points of view: the number of people who seek
comfort in alcohol, drugs, tranquilizers; the number who try to
escape their loneliness in bars; the yearning that one hears expressed among people of all walks of life for a sense of belonging,
fellowship. How can we "realize" each other more fully? How
can we become more adept where human relations are concerned? How can we become more truly human in our relations
with one another?

Human beings have at their command memory, reflection,
judgment, accumulated knowledge, awareness, insight. They can
make available to each other: support, comfort, sympathy, com-
passion, empathy, encouragement, stimulation. What do people
look for in their person-to-person contacts? What do they give?
What do they receive?

In response to a feature article on how men and women
interact with one another in the Cleveland *Plain Dealer*, I received
two long letters from two men in protest. One complained that
all women wanted to hear was that they were beautiful. The other
complained that women did not know the difference between
discussion and an argument. What serious indictments these are,
if true. They warrant examination whether one is addressing oneself to the man-woman interplay or to people-to-people interaction in general. The problem is the same: what do we want;
how do we go about getting it? Is what we are looking for appropriate; possible?

It makes a difference if our social contacts are intended to fill a vacuum, to pass the time; to speed the treadmill; to escape from ourselves—our aloneness, our loneliness. It makes a difference if what we look for in person-to-person contacts is acceptance, affirmation (support, the yardstick, the paddle); the "shoulder to weep on"; the companion-in-trouble. It makes a difference if we are looking for: understanding, involvement, participation, a sounding board for ideas. We need to examine what part of us surfaces in our contacts with relatives, with friends, with acquaintances. Is it our separateness: how we are different, distinct? Is it our dependency: where we are weak, inadequate? Is it our search for an at-oneness with another: our interests, our commitments?

And then we must consider what makes us: interesting, likable, lovable, worth being with. We must shed the fantasy that just "being" is enough (the prebirth reality). It is just not true. The people-to-people experience is a privilege. It carries a cost. It deserves and must have investment if it is to yield its maximum potential.

As we assess the end results of our people-to-people experiences, we need to consider how people fail us. Are they too self-involved to be empathic? Are they too vulnerable to the same risks—bereavement, loss, abandonment—to venture vicarious involvement? Are they themselves survivors of life-threatening crises and therefore unwilling or unable to be empathic, unwilling, unable to risk reactivated hurt? What are valid expectations in people-to-people relationships: temporary, transient, continuing, in-depth?

There are also questions to which we must address ourselves if we are to understand what happens in our person-to-person contacts: is what we want possible; is what we want available? If what we want is possible and available how do we go about achieving it?

Communication

Communication seems to be the theme of the day together with the search for togetherness. The "communication" that people seem to be striving for strikes me as another form of the search for "oneness," for the fusion that was experienced in the womb. Instead we should be striving to develop the skills that acknowledge, confirm, and extend separateness, differentness. We should be looking for that which adds to, that which expands, that which enriches the life experience, through sharing, through pooling one's individual perceptions and reactions with each other.

Communication in essence involves a process. To communicate is to transmit information, ideas, thoughts, feelings, attitudes. So often when people get together "everybody talks, nobody listens." Each one remains in his own mental cubicle untouched, unaffected by contact with another mind. Actually only the vocal cords and auditory systems have been active, not the mind. One could categorize this type of interaction as chitchat rather than communication. For communication technically speaking is additive. It should bring to the situation something that was not there before. It involves *reciprocity*; exchange. It requires involvement: "You add to my dreams, I'll add to yours." Reciprocity can involve risk. There is the risk of having one's point of view challenged; having to address oneself to a point of view different from one's own.

Genuine, involved communication is a rarity. And for good reason. Everyone cherishes his own perceptions, his own point of view, his own values. The wish to change, to grow must be greater than the wish for security for the individual to take the risk.

For the most part what we look for from each other is confirmation of our own point of view. We prefer to be like others rather than different. We look for what matches and tend to discard what differs or contradicts. We generally would rather imitate than modify. For open interaction, for communication in the truest sense there must be confidence that one's individuality will be appreciated and respected. Having one's opinions appreciated and respected carries a price. I heard it so well stated in a meeting recently. A member of the audience was taking issue with the speaker and asserted belligerently, "I have a right to my opinion." The speaker respectfully concurred. Quietly but firmly he added: "Providing you are knowledgeable and accountable." The sharing of ignorance is an imposition. It is an imposition that no one should tolerate. We can look to the comics for affirmation. It was Beetle Bailey who protested to the sergeant: "This is still a free country and I have a right to say what I think." "You're right," replied the sergeant, adding as he punched Beetle on the nose: "Of course I have a right not to hear it."

Simone de Beauvoir observes: "Men mask their depotism; women mask their cowardice." Hopefully, as the preoccupation with maleness and femaleness gives way to true peoplehood, authenticity will be the basis of communication and conversation so that the meeting of minds can lead to enrichment. Richard Schermerhorn,[11] a sociology professor at Case Western Reserve University predicted in his book *Society and Power*, that there will be a time in our society when the greatest crime will be to be a bore. This will put both men and women on their mettle. Equality—economic, social, political—will necessarily lead to psychological equality with men and women equally responsible for contributing appropriately in social interaction. Unless of course, the human species follows the pattern of mountain goats; male and female coming together only for mating.

In all social interaction we need to remember that there is a critical difference between sharing what one knows, thinks, believes and what one feels. Harvey Jackson[12] in his *The Human Side of Human Beings* puts it so very well:

I act by thought and logic.
I just feel the way I feel.
I don't confuse these separate things.
Nor wind them on one reel.

In the interest of separateness, autonomy, dignity and privacy this is a distinction that warrants high priority in our social protocol.

Psychological Equipment for Social Survival

Without the extended family, with one's best friends most likely to be strangers on the move, with the participants in one's life constantly changing, it is urgent that the human being develop an inner rootedness; an internal center of gravity that he can take with him wherever he goes. In addition to a firm sense of self, of "me-ness," there are other psychological tools that are essential to survival in a rapidly changing mobile world of ever-expanding dimensions. High in importance is *flexibility*—the capacity to change; to accommodate to the unexpected. *Intrigue with the unknown*—a sense of adventure; *a sense of wonder*—these lend challenge and excitement to the life experience. There is ample evidence (consider the under-three-year-old) that the human being comes into the world well equipped for adventure, with a keen sense of wonder. That these innate attributes are stunted or completely aborted by the age of 5 is an indictment of our nurturing and socialization processes. It might be still another indictment of industrialization which places so many pressures on nurturing adults that they do not have sufficient time and energy to foster the development of wonder and adventure in the younger generation.

Essential to the individual's psychological well-being and capacity to cope with complex and changing life conditions is *self-esteem*—a feeling of self-worth, of importance. In a society that promotes competition and comparison how does the individual establish and maintain his self-esteem? Current efforts to use the child's individual potential as the yardstick by which his achievements are measured are encouraging. They may provide the foundation on which the goal of individual autonomy can be built.

An important if not essential concomitant is learning to experience *pleasure from achievement*. As recently as April 29, 1978, the comic-strip character Ziggy was informed by his physicians, "one of the first symptoms of this new disease is a general feeling of well-being." The comics often alert us to changes that are in the offing. What a welcome change it would be to have "well-being" a goal and an expectation.

There are such simple things adults could do to help children achieve this sense of well-being. There are such simple things adults do that unwittingly destroy it. What an excellent example I experienced in a drug store just the other day. A father was shopping with his 7-year-old son. The son was buying a pack of cinnamon chewing gum. The conversation went something like this: Father to son: "That's no good." "Yes it is." "You won't like it." "Yes I will." And there the conversation ended, an impasse. The child stood his ground probably to find later that his father was right. The cost to his self-confidence, who knows? How much better it would have been had the father asked if he knew that the gum he had chosen was cinnamon and inquired if he had ever tasted it before. If there were indications that the child had not known and that he had had no experience with the taste, the father might have explained what cinnamon was like and opened the way to the child's changing his mind. The father would have been imparting knowledge instead of impugning the child's judgment. The child may still have stood by his choice, but with less risk to his feeling a failure. A lightness of touch, too, would have been helpful. A package of gum; what an excellent opportunity for the child to begin to experience, and acknowledge taste differences and his preferences. If it turned out that he didn't like it, so what? He would buy another flavor the next time. A sense of "tomorrow," a sense of the ever-changing nature of life and living, a sense of the individual's change potential, his potential for mastery should be the central and constant theme of all child-rearing, all acculturation and educational processes.

Socrates suggested that each individual develop early the ralization that he is a character in his own life story. What each should be saying to the other is: "Here I am. Read me." and, "Let me read you."

Conclusion

The single most basic need at this point in time for the human species seems to be the need for community; the need to belong. Whether this need will persist if nurturing and acculturation succeed in helping the human psyche deal with its intrinsic aloneness remains to be seen. In the meantime society is making adaptations to this current need. To substitute for the extended family there are developing communes, planned communities, condominiums that provide social and educational opportunities. There are self-help groups: parents without partners; widow-widowers; sensitivity training; encounter. Block organizations, and bingo parties provide opportunity for discussion, planning, recreation. Strangers take on the function of the extended family. Being a stranger is a point of commonality and can provide the beginning of relationships.

According to Vance Packard the average American moves 14 times in a lifetime. One out of five lives more than 1,000 miles from his birthplace. At least one-fifth of our population moves at least once a year. Eric Berne, the author of *Games People Play*, says ". . . being grounded in oneself is about the highest state a human being can achieve." With the extent of mobility Packard describes inner rootedness becomes an essential to survival. Inner rootedness requires first of all a sense of self; a sense of separateness. It requires self-awareness, self-knowledge: what one wants, what one needs, what one prefers, what one dislikes. It requires acceptance of aloneness as an intrinsic characteristic of the human estate, a characteristic completely free of any implication of helplessness or failure. Inner rootedness should carry with it the ability to create one's own challenges; one's own "touchstones to growth," one's own retreats. Coupled with autonomy, inner rootedness should make it possible for one to give without strings, to receive without being burdened by debt, to engage fully, reciprocally in growth-inspiring, growth-producing experiences.

Social instrumentation to meet the psychic needs of the human personality seems to be under way in the emergence of new lifestyles; schools without walls, education with no terminal points. Programming for the intrapsychic growth and change necessary for survival in a postindustrial global society does not exist in any conscious, deliberate, conceptualized form. Whatever efforts are being undertaken seem to be essentially intuitive, subliminal. It is urgent that they be made conscious and deliberate, and that they be made public.

Notes

1. Borden, William, *The Family Game* (New York: Quadrangle, 1972).
2. McLuhan, Marshall, *Understanding Media* (New York: McGraw-Hill, 1964), pp. 33, 39, 40, 59.

3. Eiseley, Loren, "The Cosmic Orphan," *Saturday Review/World* (February 23, 1974).

4. Cousteau, Jacques, *The Ocean World of Jacques Cousteau*, vol. 1 (New York: Duxbury Press, 1975), pp. 74–78, 96.

5. Rank, Otto, *The Trauma of Birth* (New York: Harper & Row, 1973).

6. Maltz, Maxwell, *Psycho-Cybernetics* (New York: Simon & Schuster, 1967).

7. Boulding, Kenneth, in *Learning for Tomorrow*, Alvin Toffler, ed. (New York: Random House, 1974), p. 197.

8. Schermerhorn, Richard, *Society and Power* (New York: Random House, 1961).

9. U.S. Census Report, March 1977 (Washington, D.C.: Government Printing Office).

10. O'Neill, Nena and George, *Shifting Gears* (New York: Avon, 1975).

11. Schermerhorn, 1961.

12. Jackson, Harvey, *The Human Side of Human Beings.*

Bibliography

Clarke, Arthur C., *The Promise of Space* (New York: Harper & Row, 1968).

DeBono, Edward, *Think Tank* (Toronto: Think Tank Corp., 1973).

Goodman, Paul, *Communitas* (New York: Vintage, 1947).

May, Rollo, *The Courage to Create* (New York: Norton, 1975).

Toffler, Alvin, *Future Shock* (New York: Bantam, 1971).

CHAPTER 6

Our Bicameral Brain and Psychotherapy: A Proposal*

Folk wisdom provided the clue and cue to the exploration upon which this exposition is based. Current brain research has provided the scientific frame of reference. A continuing search for more effective, efficient procedures in mental health intervention has provided the impetus and the daring for the proposals that emerge from this excursion into brain anatomy. For the clinical social worker this is far afield indeed.

As I reviewed Freud's professional history, the lines from T. S. Eliot's *Four Quartets*[1] came to mind:

> We shall not cease from exploration
> And the end of all our exploring
> Will be to arrive where we started
> And know the place for the first time.

Our new technology is providing empirical evidence for many of Freud's theories on brain anatomy and organization, and on brain energy flow. This empirical evidence warrants our consideration.

---

* Presented at the 18th Annual I=CAPP Conference, Vancouver, Canada, June 20, 1979.

Introduction

Aristotle believed that consciousness or thought was located just above the heart, and that the brain was the cooling system of the body, not subject to touch or injury. It was not until the eighteenth century that it was established that the brain was the locus of thought, the receptor of sensation, the instigator of action: mental, motor, emotional.[2] It was hypothesized then that brain structures could be modified by use or disuse. But it was not until the 1950s that there was empirical evidence through experimentation with rats that the brain is plastic, that it can be affected significantly by conditions that enrich, impoverish or involve stress. Human research since 1960 has drawn attention to the effect of subjective experience upon the functioning of the brain. From this research rich insights have already accumulated on such issues as language development, cognitive processes and brain functioning in different states of consciousness.[3]

It was at the end of the nineteenth century that it was recognized that the human nervous system consisted of a network of electrical circuits.[4] By the beginning of the twentieth century electronic instruments made it possible to establish empirically the fact of transmission via the neural network. In 1925, Lord Adrian of Cambridge, England, made the first electrical recordings of the activity of individual nerve fibers. It is ventured that his findings may prove to be a universal law as important as Newton's laws of motion.[5]

On the issue of psychic energy, it was in 1833 that Gustav Theodor Fechner suggested that mental phenomena could be viewed in the context of nervous energy similar to physical energy. Freud in his preanalytic period devoted much time to the development of a theoretical model based on brain anatomy and nervous energy. In 1895, in a rough draft of "Project for a Scientific Psychology," he posed the theory of energy flow, distribution and quantity in a hypothetical structural concept of the brain. He spoke of the ego as an organization of neurons with a reservoir of energy available at all times to exercise control over incoming stimuli and subjecting them to reality assessment and testing. Sigmund Exner spoke in terms of brain centers where pain is experienced and of the channeling of energy. Pierre Janet spoke in terms of psychological debts, and the need perhaps for a moratorium when too much energy has been expended, when emotional reserves have been depleted. He postulated too that there were psychological millionaires, i.e., people with abundant psychic energy.[6]

What has been generally acknowledged through the centuries is that the human brain is the most intricate and powerful of all the works of nature known to man. The first major breakthrough in the study of the brain was made in the last quarter of the nineteenth century when it was discovered that there was a correlation between clinical observations and brain anatomy. The period 1940–74 has seen a burgeoning of knowledge on brain functioning never before experienced, at least in the period of recorded history.

Theoretical Frame of Reference

Characteristics

The concept of the unconscious has existed for many centuries. During the eighteenth and nineteenth centuries, the concept was subjected to experimental and clinical research. The personality theorists who bridged the nineteenth and twentieth centuries viewed the unconscious as having many specific characteristics. Freud saw the unconscious as a special realm with its own will, desires, modes of expression and mental mechanisms unique unto itself, i.e., not elsewhere operative. He talked about an unconscious system and a conscious system, separate and distinct one from the other, almost like two separate human beings. He talked about energy output and "circuitous pathways" through which frustrated desires seek gratification.[7] He postulated that there was a topography of the brain and that one might be able to locate the spot where regressions occurred: also that there was a channel from the unconscious to the conscious. He ventured that the conscious might be located in the cortex of the brain and the unconscious in the lower brain center.[8]

Theodor Lipps, in the late 1890s described the unconscious as the basis of psychic life and being "like a chain of undersea mountains, in which only the peaks emerge, representing the conscious." He saw the unconscious as having potentially tyrannical power sufficient to bring the individual to ruin, and all without conscious awareness of what was happening.

The unconscious has been recognized generally as having no sense of objective reality, no concern with time or sequence, and as having at its command boundless energy. It can create its own reality to which it holds tenaciously, and which it can bring into play without regard for appropriateness or consequence.

The concept of the unconscious to be used in this exposition refers to those mental experiences that occur outside the realm of conscious awareness, and are essentially inaccessible to cognitive, rational processes of the mind. I concur with those theorists who believe the unconscious to have its locus in the right hemisphere of the brain. This accedes to its evolutionary seniority over the left hemisphere. Its evolutionary seniority provides rationale for the fact that the unconscious has at its command vast stores of powerful energy. The source of this energy remains a mystery.

Content

There have been many theories as to the source of the content stored in the unconscious, and so resistant to outside influence. Many theorists refer to ancestral inheritance transmitted through the genes as a part of each individual's unconscious, a part of his innate equipment. Some believe that stored in the unconscious are the memories of previous lives the individual and/or the species has experienced. Other sources of content in the unconscious are believed to be subjective and objective life experiences, the permissions, restrictions and admonitions that accrue during the nurturing and socialization process, the productions of each individual's perceptual and affective mechanisms—his own very special brand of fantasy and imagination, of wishes and fears, or the brand consistent with the specific cultural milieu in which he grows. There is growing empirical evidence that the intrauterine experience is rich in sensation—response to light, to sound, to movement. In my womb imprint theory I am postulating deeply embedded intrapsychic patterning that affects afterbirth expectations.

What is not known, and may never be known, is what determines content selection, content storage and retrieval. Most sobering of all is the possibility being posited as a result of current research that the content in the unconscious may not be subject to change or eradication. Our years of clinical experience demonstrate that change is difficult. Empirical research is suggesting that perhaps we have undertaken the impossible when we try to change or eradicate what the unconscious guards so zealously.

Exploration

During the period 1880–1900 many methods were developed and tested for exploring the unconscious. Among the most significant of these was the work of three pioneers in dream investigation: Scherner, Maury, and Hervey de Saint Denis. Their findings led to the elaboration of dream theory which later influenced the work of Freud and Jung. Techniques were developed for the observation, modification and mastery of dreams. It was found that one could easily train oneself to remember dreams. Maury demonstrated that one could produce dreams as well as influence them by diet, atmospheric conditions and sensory stimulation. Hervey de St. Denis demonstrated how one could master one's dreams. The methodology, however, was so complex that it drew few adherents.

The word-association test was developed by Francis Galton. In the 1870s Cambridge University undertook the study of clairvoyance. In the 1890s Theodore Flournoy (1854–1920) undertook the study of mediums at the University of Geneva. When dealing with subconscious fixed ideas, Janet tried association, substitution, interpretation of possible symbolic implications, distractions, automatic writing, automatic talking, crystal gazing. He also tried electrical stimulation and massage.[9]

In 1840, Spiritism came to the fore. With impetus from the telegraph, it reached all parts of the world within 15 years of its inception. Spiritism led to the development of the new science: Parapsychology.

In 1882, the Society for Psychical Research was established in England. Automatic writing, introduced by Spiritists was taken over by scientists as a method for exploring the unconscious. Jean-Martin Carcot (1835–1893), a neurologist of reknown, believed that faith healing, i.e., healing under the auspices of religion, might have significance in the understanding of therapeutic processes. Other approaches to the unconscious during the eighteenth and nineteenth centuries included exorcism, artificially induced sleep and hypnotism.[10]

The entire nineteenth century was preoccupied with the coexistence of the two minds (the right and the left hemispheres of the brain) and their relationship to each other within the context of the human personality. Each hemisphere, sometimes referred to as layers, was recognized as having its own characteristics, its own processing pattern, and system of memory storage. Each was seen as operating simultaneously, autonomously and as competing with the other for dominance in controlling the individual's behavior and reactions.[11]

Early neurologists who concerned themselves with the functioning of the two hemispheres assessed the left as being more important because of its involvement with speech. They concentrated their efforts on this hemisphere. Only since 1967 have psychologists, neurosurgeons and neurophysiologists given attention to the exploration of the right hemisphere.

Work with epileptics and with persons suffering brain damage due to accidents or strokes has revealed that

- In 90% of the subjects, the faculty of speech is centered in the left hemisphere. The right hemisphere has the capacity to sing, to write poetry, but not to rhyme.
- The left hemisphere organizes over time; the right over space without consideration of time and sequence. The right hemisphere seems to have special aptitude in visiospatial tasks. Its judgment of depth and of spatial relationships is superior to that of the left hemisphere.
- The left hemisphere is cognitive, logical; the right, intuitive,

imaginative. The left does better with writing; the right, with drawing.

- The left hemisphere analyzes the whole into its component parts; the right sees the whole.[12]
- Research findings are pointing to the possibility that male and female brains are organized differently. The brain of the female seems to be somewhat less distinctly lateralized than that of the male. Women suffering damage to the left hemisphere are known to suffer less speech impairment than men.
- Both hemispheres seem to understand language, but the right does not have the capacity for speech.
- There is a space in the right hemisphere which seems to have no function. Jaynes suggests this space may have been reserved for the "gods." It occurs to me that his space, if not reserved for the "gods," if unoccupied, may be available for the next development of man.[13]

Marilyn Fergusson[14] postulates that the separateness of right and left hemispheres may vary in individuals. The cleavage between the two may vary in size, thickness, penetrability. Interhemisphere activity may vary with mood, and circumstance. She suggests that a "new kind of light," not "more" of what we have had, is necessary to increase our understanding. The problem facing researchers is their own deeply embedded perceptions, which are always a hindrance to the pristine approach to familiar phenomena. According to Fergusson, there is nothing in current research that suggests that what is stored in the right hemisphere can be erased. She suggests that perhaps one day children all over the world will offer their dreams at the breakfast table, intrigued with the creativeness, the imagination of the right hemisphere, rather than being frightened by hidden significance.

Janov, in the same vein, has suggested that human mentality may develop to the point that there is no unconscious. Both hemispheres will be privy to the content of the other, and each will be available to pursue what the individual undertakes to do. The two hemispheres, functioning in harmony, each complementing the other, each contributing its own unique capability, makes it possible for the individual to function at maximum capacity.

Practical Implications

Theorists involved with right-left hemisphere activity have suggested that there may be individuals who are right hemisphere dominated. These may be the artists, the musicians, the mathematicians, the writers of fiction, of poetry. We know, for instance, that people who have suffered left hemisphere damage can sing, but not speak, can write poetry, but not rhyme. People who are adept at jigsaw puzzles, who have mechanical aptitude, may be right hemisphere dominant. There may be individuals who are left hemisphere dominated. These may be the theoreticians, the individuals who are adept at thinking but not at feeling; the people who can reason but not imagine. There may be people who have equal access to both hemispheres. There may be individuals in whom right hemisphere interference occurs chronically when the individual is under stress, and those where the interfering aspects of the right hemisphere gain dominance only in acute crises.

Alcohol, drugs, physical and mental exhaustion invite right hemisphere takeover. The mantra, repetitive prayers, incantations, rhythmic, repetitive sounds like the voodoo drums, repetitive body movements as in primitive dancing, concentrating attention on physical sensations, are devices that disconnect the left and right hemispheres, giving dominance to the latter. Movies such as *The Exorcist, Rosemary's Baby*, provide fodder for the right hemisphere, give it nurturance, reinforce its powers, provide the climate for yielding dominance to it. The appeal that such dramatic enterprises have for people may be a clue to the extent to which people prefer right hemisphere to left hemisphere activity. The crucial question for those attracted to these experiences is what is the effect: do they increase creativity; do they increase disruptive energy, energy that interferes with disciplined, purposive goal-directed activity? Individuals who have difficulty keeping right hemisphere activity under control, who find that right hemisphere activity interferes with, interrupts, inhibits left hemisphere performance, should avoid all activities that indulge, support, nurture right hemisphere activity and power if what they want for themselves is to maximize their potential.

Personality theorists, like physicists, deal with phenomena that cannot be touched, tasted, seen, yet are real. Physicists have available meters, recordings from which they can draw inferences which they cannot explain. What instruments the personality theorist has are primitive indeed in comparison with the complexity of the psychic phenomena with which he is expected to deal. The most that either the physicist or the personality theorist can do is develop models which aid in exploration and can provide the arena for testing.

The theory of relativity required of scientists a way of thinking to accommodate new data not taken into account by Newton. Similarly, the bicameral, neural network concept of the brain requires a new look at the human personality, at patterns of intrapsychic functioning.[15] Serving as the backdrop for this new look is the fact that there is ample evidence that the "mature, well developed individual" has access to both hemispheres of the brain and is able to engage either or both as is appropriate to the task at hand. It is reported that George Eliot, for instance, wrote letters to her unconscious instructing it on what she wanted it to do. Bertrand Russell is said to have ordered his unconscious to work underground while he went on to other things, i.e., after he had done all the work he believed necessary for the task he had undertaken.

For practitioners like ourselves concerned with people who have difficulty coping; who have difficulty accommodating to reality; who experience dysfunctional reactions, cognitive, affective and behavioral, the persistent, perennial question over the years has been and continues to be why, and what can we do about it.

The demands of a rapidly changing, highly mobile world are taxing the capabilities of the human being as he is currently endowed, genetically, sociologically. The degree of distress is reflected in the burgeoning rate of suicide especially among young people. The extent of the distress is reflected in the fact that Americans consume 27 million pounds of aspirin a year; 19 million individuals suffer chronic depression; 70 million Americans drink alcohol; 1½ million are admitted to mental hospitals a year.[16]

Development of more economical, more effective less time-consuming interventive techniques is urgent. Perhaps the bicameral, neural network frame of reference has possibilities in this direction. Let us consider it.

The Neural Network Approach to Intrapsychic Intervention

In the neural network approach to intrapsychic intervention certain traditional concepts play no part. Among these are the concepts of instinct, impulses, inhibition, repressions. In their stead are the concepts of appropriateness, relevance, pertinence, with reality the determining factor in each of these considerations. There is no concern with content of right hemisphere involvement; no concern with memory retrieval. Dreams are considered as providing clues to what the right hemisphere is dealing with— archaic fantasies, fantasies of magical power, preoccupation with destruction, with death. They provide information as to the areas in which the left hemisphere needs knowledge, understanding, reinforcement. What is in the right hemisphere is accepted "as is," plus the fact that the right hemisphere has a right to perceive and believe as it does. What it does not have is the right to impose its perceptions, its beliefs, upon the left hemisphere. It is a jurisdictional issue. If one wants to be a logical, rational, reality-oriented individual, one must designate the left hemisphere of the brain as the part of the brain that has authority to control and to direct. The overseer or guardian of hemisphere dominance is the ego. The ego is the decision-making part of the human personality. Many personality theorists besides Freud have talked in terms of the ego as the gatekeeper, the guardian, the overseer that determines which stimuli shall be admitted where, and to what end. In *Beyond the Pleasure Principle*, Freud spoke of strengthening the ego in its task as gatekeeper through clarification of values, priorities and goals. What Freud referred to as "manifold resistances" might well be seen in terms of insecurity, confusion, ambivalence about values, priorities, goals.

The ultimate goal in the neural network approach is to bring the right and left hemispheres of the brain into harmony with each other: that they be "friends" and be able to work together, each complementing the other, each bringing to bear its specialness, its uniqueness of skill, content and wisdom.

The view of the brain as a neural network with one or more control centers suggests that anatomically the human species is equipped for change. With a nervous system capable of development—capable of making new neural connections where the established ones are inadequate, malfunctioning or injured, there can be compensation for, or adaptation to, deficiencies caused by accident or a condition at birth. There can be new neural connections to deal with new life circumstances.

The operational characteristics of each of the two hemispheres of the brain must be taken into account as we consider the growth and the adaptive potential of the brain. Namely, each hemisphere has its own processing pattern and memory storage system: each hemisphere has specialized functions, though they are not necessarily mutually exclusive, and each hemisphere seeks to gain dominance over the other in influencing and controlling the individual's behavior. In the early part of the twentieth century, Freud and his colleagues recognized that the right hemisphere (the unconscious, nonrational part of the human personality) was powerful. It had seniority over the left hemisphere as far as evolutionary development was concerned. It had a vast reservoir of energy at its command for use, not necessarily in the best interest of the individual. As Theodor Lipps put it in the 1890s, the unconscious, with its "tyrannical power," could bring an individual to "ruin." As clinicians, we know only too well how true this is.

Charles Tart[17] observed that Western societies have focused attention on the development of the left hemisphere. They have done little to educate or modify right hemisphere functioning. In fact, he does not believe we have the procedures, the techniques or the knowledge to influence right hemisphere functioning. It was Tart's observation on this last point, the possibility that we do not know and that we do not have the techniques for dealing with the right hemisphere, that started me on the road to this exposition.

We may assume from all descriptive evidence that the right

hemisphere houses the unconscious. In it, therefore, is deeply embedded the residuals of genetic inheritance (what Carl Jung calls the archetypes), the archaic fantasies, fantasies of magical thinking and magical power of childhood. Jaynes' view of the right hemisphere as the abode of the "gods" suggests a possible source of the tremendous potency and persistence of these archaic constructs.

Personality theorists over the years have agreed that what the unconscious chooses for storage and retrieval is outside the range of conscious control. Often the material it chooses to retain has not even been processed in the conscious (left hemisphere). The reasons that enter into the selection, the influences that lead to activation or retrieval are not known. They often defy even inference or conjecture. They are solely, completely, under right hemisphere control and domination. The left hemisphere often is not privy or conscious, or in accord with, the content or the process.

Two assumptions undergird what follows. First, that we do not know what, why and how the unconscious (or the right hemisphere) perceives and stores what it does. Second, we do not know what brings unconscious content into play.

It was during the early weeks following my husband's death that I posed to one of my youngest friends, aged 85, who had been widowed 15 years before: What does one do when panic strikes? She stated very simply: "Stop what you are doing and do something else." It worked. It worked not only in stilling the panic. It brought to an end the compulsive, treadmill, broken-record thinking that invaded sleep. It brought to an end the surging force that would virtually catapult me out of my chair in the middle of an interview when the time overlapped my usual pattern of being at home. How come? What was the dynamic that operated here to bring destructive, purposeless, inappropriate behavior under control?

The exploring I was doing on my womb-imprint theory led me into brain research, into a study of brain anatomy, into the material on neural networks and the control centers of the brain. Thence to a theory of intervention and some specific procedures. The procedures presented are intended to bring under control only those aspects of right hemisphere activity that interfere with left hemisphere functioning. The creative, intuitive capabilities of the right hemisphere, all of its wealth of imagination, its special aptitudes with numbers and spatial relationships are neither under scrutiny nor in question. Our concern is with the right hemisphere when it uses archaic thinking, fantasies of magical power, dire predictions of impending doom to interfere with the logical, rational, reality-related activities of the left hemisphere. Personality observers and theorists have known for centuries the destructive power that resides in that part of the human personality that is beyond conscious, rational control. It is to divest the right hemisphere of that power that these procedures are directed.

Procedures for Neural Network Intervention

Neural network intervention is three-pronged. It involves: (1) bringing disruptive right hemisphere activity under control; (2) reinforcing left hemisphere activity; and (3) strengthening the psychic decision-making agent commonly referred to as the ego or the will.

Bringing the Right Hemisphere Under Control

There are three steps to bringing the right hemisphere activity under control. The first step is awareness. The individual must be alert to right hemisphere intrusion. Day-dreaming, having the mind wandering to things not pertinent to the task at hand, being distracted by sights and sounds not related to what one is doing, wondering about whether one is doing well instead of concentrating on doing what one is doing as well as one can (being judge and jury of one's current performance); these are right hemisphere maneuvers to interfere with left hemisphere activity. They must be brought under control if the left hemisphere is to proceed with its task. Right hemisphere activity is persistent. It tends to be compulsive, once it starts it is difficult to stop. It tends to be repetitive, much like the broken record or the treadmill. It tends to be circular, i.e., it goes nowhere, except around and around in its established groove.

Once the individual is aware of right hemisphere intrusion, he must quickly and firmly stop it. Here a conversation between the right and left hemisphere can take place with the left hemisphere asserting control: "This is no time to be thinking about those things; we'll think about that later . . ." affirming the importance of the task at hand and the individual's determination to do it. The corpus callosum is the organ through which communication between the two hemispheres is channeled.

If the right hemisphere activity is persistent, unresponsive to the direction or admonition of the left hemisphere, the individual must stop what he is doing and do something else. The mind, it has been established, can concentrate on only one thing at a time. Stopping the activity and doing something else interrupts the concentration, stops the flow of energy from right to left hemisphere. It is like closing a valve. If the procedure is invoked quickly, before right hemisphere activity is entrenched, and consistently, i.e., whenever it intrudes, there is the possibility that the nerve fibers transmitting the energy from the right to the left hemisphere may atrophy, much as do muscles when they are not used.[18] (Research being conducted on the newborn has revealed that "neural structures present at birth will disappear if not used during the first months of life.")[19]

The principle behind this three-step technique is not new, nor is it unique. Alvin Mahrer, in delineating humanistic therapy, describes the focusing of attention on desired behavior, ignoring undesirable behavior. The result is that the undesirable activity ceases to operate. He points out that the procedure differs from behavioral modification in that it does not involve either repetition or reward. Its focus is on the development of new behavior consistent with the individual's goals.[20] Charles Tart describes what he calls the "mindfulness technique." It requires self-observation, the development of awareness of what is happening.

The process of self-observation and awareness serves to "dismantle" those "structures of the mind" from which the undesirable behavior emanated. The result: the undesirable behavior weakens and ultimately disappears, becomes inoperative, even in the presence of old stimuli.[21] Tart views the mindfulness technique as of limited usefulness if the behavior under consideration is so integral a part of the individual's acculturated personality, so much a part of his defense system, that it is beyond the scope of awareness.

In the neural network approach all that is necessary is that the individual be aware that he is unable to do what he set out to do. This would be the cue that he is experiencing right hemisphere interference and he would proceed to bring it under control without knowing or needing to know the nature of the interference or the reason for it. To spot the interference: that is the task. Only if the interference persists, only if the individual is not able to bring it under control, would one need to move on to steps 2 and 3 mentioned above. And before moving on to steps 2 and 3 one would need to check out energy level: is it possible that the individual may have been overextending himself so that he does not have available the energy necessary to buttress left hemisphere activity in its struggle with the right hemisphere? If so, was the overextension within his control, or was it response to external conditions beyond his control? Another factor that needs to be checked out is the matter of stress. Was the individual under stress that was energy-draining? Was the stress internal, external? Was the stress within his power to control? If both energy expenditure and stress factors were within his power to control and he did not, one may well be dealing with lacunae, gaps in motivation, fear in the face of the unknown, in the face of a new awareness of risks. With the realization that one can be in full control of one's life if one chooses to be (this is what the right-left hemisphere concept seems to make clear), then one faces ending of the therapeutic relationship. With improvement happening so quickly, and consolidation within the conscious control of the individual, readiness for ending becomes an issue and can be a deterrent to effective use of the procedure.

In the five months (December 1978–April 1979) that I have been using the neural network procedure, I have seen within the space of four interviews the freeing of potential that had been inhibited by archaic worries of aggression slow to modification in six months of my usual treatment procedures. Treatment ended with the individual having applied for, and received, a job at the highest rung of her potential and experience.

Judy, a young lady new to treatment, was suffering depression bordering on withdrawal due to an unsuccessful love affair. Within a period of five interviews, Judy was functioning maximally in school and reaching out most successfully in the social arena. As she ended her contacts with me, there was vitality, exuberance, confidence that she was in control of her life.

Marlene and I had been working together for about a year. Only once in that period of time did M. venture out of her lethargy, her feeling of futility, and consider what she might do with her life over and above what she was doing. When I explained to M. the new procedure, she became very troubled. She wouldn't be able to use the new procedure because she was never aware of when her right hemisphere intruded or took over. If that was true, what we would have to do, I explained, was to develop her abilities at self-observation and self-awareness. When M. came in the next week, she was exuberant. Not only had she begun to be aware of the activity of her right hemisphere, but she had remembered some crucial experiences in her life which had been completely forgotten. In these new-found memories lay a possible explanation for her apathy, her cynicism, her marginal performance in school and work. For the first time in her 25 years, M. felt she was in control of her life. She had made some new friends, she had begun to learn how to ski, and she had joined a dance group. What was even more, she was beginning to look forward to considering work that would have more challenge in it for her.

Today, five months after she was introduced to the new procedure, Marlene heads a department in which she had been employed in lesser capacities for about a year and a half. She is in charge of purchasing, staff development and staff management. She is engaging eagerly in her new responsibilities, the new challenges, and with an interest in learning which she has never experienced before.

Using the neural network procedures, Bill found himself after twelve interviews able to set aside archaic fantasies of omnipotence, magical power and rivalry with his dad which had plagued him most of his 25 years (and for which he had had the usual treatment for about a year before). The abdominal distress which had been chronic was gradually dissipating, even though the externals in his life situation were full of the unknown. He began to experience for the first time the satisfaction that goes along with being a disciplined, responsible adult; the relief of being able to accord and benefit by the knowledge and experience of his seniors. And most impressive of all, Bill was able to allow himself the pleasures of being a learner. What a relief it was, not to be burdened by having to know it all. How exciting it was to consider what more there was for him to learn and master as life went on.

Jennifer had still another experience. After just one application of the three-step procedure she found that for the first time in her life her mind was at rest. She was comfortable with who and what she was. The energy that was suddenly available to her was phenomenal in quantity and quality. She was able to do so many things, so many different things, and with energy to spare. Never before had she experienced this. Of course, she was afraid to trust it, afraid it wouldn't last. There were so many things she wanted to do. Finally she was convinced that she had the capability to do whatever she decided she wanted to do.

But it was 10-year-old Debra who gave me the most graphic, dramatic description of the issues involved.

Debra and her two brothers had been subject of many parent guidance sessions. For four years her mother had wanted me to see D. I had always considered under 12-year-olds beyond the range of my expertise, and I had had ample evidence over the years that D.'s problems could be managed through parent guidance. Suddenly, a year and a half ago, with a divorce and a major housing move pending, D.'s problems took on an urgency that I believed required direct intervention. Since I knew the family so well, it seemed to me the most effective, economical procedure was that I see D. Her mother was delighted. I saw D. five times. We discussed penis envy, the oedipal, and how these fantasies were affecting D.'s relationships with her younger brother and with her friends. Five interviews seemed to be all D. needed. Things went better at home and with her relationships. She no longer had to take quantities of candy to school every day to distribute among her friends. She made the move to the new neighborhood and the new school without incident. She made new friends, and without the aid of candy.

In January 1979, a year and a half later, D. told her mother she thought she ought to come in to talk with me. She was having trouble falling asleep and her dreams were very scary. Her mother suggested that she call me, which she proceeded to do promptly. D. made sure that her mother would be waiting for her downstairs instead of in the waiting room, which is not soundproof. She then proceeded to bring me up to date. A more complete review of what had happened since we last met would be difficult to imagine. She touched on all areas which had given her concern.

When she finished, I told her I had learned some things since I had seen her last which I would like to tell her about. I started to tell her about the left and right hemispheres of the brain. She stopped me. She knew all about that; her mother had told her. I then proceeded to apply this split brain concept to the problems of sleeping and bad dreams that D. was experiencing. D. was her usual attentive self, asking for clarification as she found it necessary.

When she came in a week later, she told me she was better. Getting to sleep was not quite so difficult, and her dreams were not quite so scary. But said D. defiantly, "I don't want to give up what's in the right hemisphere of my brain. I am in a creative writing class and I don't want to give that up." I assured her we weren't going to do anything to interfere with the creative part of her right hemisphere. All we wanted to do was to stop the right hemisphere from doing the things that interfered with what the left hemisphere wanted to do. Mused D.: "You mean the two sides of my brain should be friends?" I agreed.

D. chattered on for a few moments, and then confided that her teacher had scolded her because she had been talking in class instead of listening. "That was the right side of my brain," D. explained to me. I was curious. I wondered what would happen if D. did not allow the right side of her brain to do that. D.'s face clouded. Words tumbled. I had never before known D. to stutter. She took a deep breath and stated soberly: "I would be very smart. I would be very smart in math and literature." "And what would be wrong with that?" I asked. Without hesitating, D. asserted: "My friends would hate me." I had to concur. That might very well happen.

Alvin Mahrer points out most graphically that if one becomes a self-actualizer, one was very likely to become persona non grata among one's friends and relatives.[22] I believed it was important for D. to know that what she said was true. That was one of the risks. But I thought she and I could figure out a way that D. could be very bright and still have friends.

D. told her dad that she was seeing me. He was livid. He didn't want me to meddle in his daughter's life. He ordered D. not to see me. He threatened me with court action. D. in the next interview was worried. I felt that D. and I had probably done all we needed to do. If she continued to have trouble, her mother and I would figure out a way of helping her. It would be up to her to let her mother know what was troubling her. That was fine with D.

One month later, the mother had her regular conference with D.'s teachers. Their reports were unbelievable. Not only had D.'s academic performance skyrocketed, but her relationships with her friends had taken on a scope and a dimension they had never had before. They wanted to know what had happened to account for all of this. Incredible to be sure. Accountable, and worthy of attention and consideration.

With D. it was not necessary to establish a procedure for bringing the right hemisphere activity under control. She needed only to understand the issue and to decide what she wanted to do about it. With adults, I find that identifying the issues is not enough. They want, and apparently need, to know what to do about what is: How can they bring right hemisphere activity under control? What must they do to strengthen the left hemisphere? How can they reinforce the ego in its task as gatekeeper or guardian?

Most of the situations in which I have applied neural network technique have required only one major application of the three-step procedure, plus an occasional alert and reminder in passing as old patterns reassert themselves. However, there have been two situations to date where the three-step procedure has worked only sporadically. What has emerged is that each of these individuals faced major problems in family relationships if they were to achieve full autonomy and self-actualization. They are ambivalent about their goal of self-fulfillment, reaching their highest potential. They are not quite ready to take the risk. Until they are ready, it is clear they will continue to permit right hemisphere interference with left hemisphere performance. There is the possibility, of course, that they may never be willing to take the risk. In that event, it is likely that they will fall short of reaching their maximum potential. They may always have to settle for something less than their highest goals and dreams, although their innate capability is there, as it always has been.

Clinicians are well-versed in steps 2 and 3: *reinforcing the left hemisphere*, and *strengthening the ego* using one or more of the known, and constantly evolving, techniques in mental health intervention. I do not believe that elaboration of the issues involved in these processes is necessary for the audience to whom this exposition is addressed. Suffice it to say that for the neural network approach to be effective, the left hemisphere may need reinforcement in the perception of objective reality, in establishing what has been mastered, what needs to be mastered, and how to achieve mastery. It may need practice with logic, with exercising judgment, with clarification of values, priorities, and goals. Similarly, the ego as the decision-making agent governing the stimuli that enter each of the two hemispheres of the brain may need reinforcement on such issues as rights, risks, and in considering options and the costs involved. Conflict, confusion, ambivalence, can interfere with the ego's performance as gatekeeper, guardian, overseer of the interaction between the right and left hemispheres of the brain, and render complementarity between the two hemispheres impossible.

To become a fully functioning adult in an age-appropriate sense requires determination, commitment, and readiness to be responsible in the assessment of what one knows, what one knows how to do, and what one needs to know, and responsibility in reality assessment and in the use of judgment in the management of one's life experience and one's relationships.

Summary

The neural network approach to psychotherapy introduces an anatomical base to functional disorders. It may bring into question such traditional constructs as personality, impulses, instincts. The neural network approach dispenses with concern about memory content, memory retrieval, recapitulation of trauma. Its focus is pragmatic. It is specific: Is the individual's behavior appropriate to objective reality? Is it consistent with his values? Is it valid, taking into account his abilities and limitations, his obligations and opportunities? These are issues that fall within left hemisphere jurisdiction. They are issues with which the right hemisphere does not concern itself.

The right hemisphere is concerned only with what it wants. It wants what it wants when it wants it, without regard for time, relevance, or availability. It does not concern itself with objective reality, with values, goals, or skills. Should the ego, which is the guardian or coordinator of the two hemispheres, be indecisive in its management of stimuli, the right hemisphere may well gain control, using its vast store of energy to override the energy and power of the left hemisphere with devastating results to the individual's plans. The three-step procedure for bringing the right hemisphere under control of the left hemisphere is simple. If it is applied quickly, firmly, and consistently, it stops the energy flow from the right to left hemisphere, bringing the compulsive right hemisphere activity under control and releasing vast quantities of energy for use in pursuance of left hemisphere activities. The ultimate goal is to bring an end to all right hemisphere interference with left hemisphere activity so that the right and left hemispheres are partners instead of rivals or antagonists, able to bring to all life activities the special attributes and skills with which each is endowed.

The three-step procedure is amazingly effective with those individuals who are committed to achieving autonomy, authenticity, accountability, and actualization. To what extent it can be used with individuals whose reality testing is flawed remains to be explored and tested.

Notes

1. Eliot, T. S., "Four Quartets," in *The Complete Poems and Plays* (New York: Harcourt Brace, 1952), p. 145.
2. Asimov, Isaac, *The Human Brain* (Boston: Houghton Mifflin, 1964), p. 3.
3. Wolman, Benjamin B., ed., *International Encyclopedia of Psychiatry, Psy-*

chology and Neurology, vol. 10 (New York: Van Nostrand Reinhold, 1977), pp. 401–430.

4. Asimov, op. cit.

5. Calder, Nigel, *The Mind of Man* (New York: Viking, 1970), p. 29.

6. Ellenberger, Henri, *The Discovery of the Unconscious* (New York: Basic Books, 1970), p. 477.

7. Freud, Sigmund, *A General Introduction to Psychoanalysis* (New York: Permabooks, 1935), pp. 222–444.

8. Jones, Ernest, *The Life and Work of Sigmund Freud* (New York: Basic Books, 1955), p. 323.

9. Ellenberger, op. cit., pp. 371–374.

10. Ibid., pp. 98–168.

11. Corballis, Michael, and Beale, Ivan, *The Psychology of the Left and Right* (Hillsdale, N.J.: Erlbaum, 1976), pp. 58–61.

12. Fergusson, Marilyn, *The Brain Revolution* (New York: Taplinger, 1975), pp. 182–183.

13. Jaynes, Julian, *The Origin of Consciousness in the Breakdown of the Bicameral Mind* (Boston: Houghton Mifflin, 1976), pp. 339–344.

14. Fergusson, op. cit.

15. Targ, Russell, and Puthoff, Harold, *Mind-Reach: Scientists Look at Psychic Ability* (New York: Creative Enterprises, 1977).

16. Federal Register, February 23, 1978, Youth Development Bureau, Department of Health, Education and Welfare, Washington, D.C.

17. Tart, Charles, *States of Consciousness* (New York: Dutton, 1975), pp. 281–232.

18. Wolman, op. cit., p. 407.

19. Bower, T. G. R., *A Primer of Infant Development* (San Francisco: Freeman, 1977), p. 159.

20. Mahrer, Alvin, *Experiencing* (New York: Brunner/Mazel, 1978), p. 569.

21. Tart, op. cit.

22. Mahrer, op. cit., p. 579.

Bibliography

Blakemore, Colin, *Mechanics of the Mind* (Cambridge: Cambridge University Press, 1976).

Brown, Barbara B., "The New Mind," *Psychology Today* (August 1974), pp. 83–112.

Pines, Maya, *The Brain Changers* (New York: Harcourt Brace Jovanovich, 1973).

Sagan, Carl, *The Dragons of Eden* (New York: Random House, 1977), p. 170.

Van Over, Raymond, *Unfinished Man* (New York: World Publishing, 1972).

CHAPTER 7

Loss and Retrieval: How Spouses Handle the Loss of a Partner: A Neutral Network Approach*

*I feared the day would come
And braced myself with
    studied
Artifice against the hurt.
It came
With sharp directed thrust.
There is no solace anywhere.*

Introduction

The behaviorist looks for cause-effect; the phenomenologist, for reason and intent. The newest intervention, holography looks for the transformations that are involved in moving from one domain in the brain to another.

According to the *International Encyclopedia of Psychiatry, Psychology, Neurology* (1977) the most firmly established findings of modern neurology are those related to hemisphere specialization.[1] It was Roger Sperry of the California Institute of

---

* Presented at the 19th Annual I-CAPP Conference, New Orleans, June, 1980.

Technology who discovered that if the corpus callosum which connects the right and left hemispheres of the brain is severed, the individual is left with two minds, two separate spheres of consciousness, each independent of and indifferent to the other. It is only since 1950 that:

- The significance of the corpus callosum has been realized.
- Evidence is accumulating that some brain states are more conducive to learning than others.
- One may be able to help individuals produce specific mental states at will.
- It has been known that there are pain and pleasure centers in the brain and that these may be accessible to conscious control through specific procedures.[2]

Through our sophisticated technology we now have empirical evidence of Freud's assumptions that psychic structure can be modified by experience and that dreaming involves a specific state of neural activity.[3] We have empirical evidence that the human nervous system consists of a network of electrical circuits,[4] and that this neural network is actively involved in the psychological phenomena that make up human experience.

What we need now, says Kenneth R. Pelletier, is "a balance between scientific inquiry concerning neurophysiology and the mapping of phenomenology of consciousness through disciplined introspection."[5] It is in this spirit and with this intent that the following exposition is undertaken.

Loss

Loss is to the human psyche what physical injury is to the body. The body has a way of localizing injury, viral or cellular. There are antibodies to fight infection. There are forces that encapsulate the injury or infection so that the invading agents do not generalize to the total body structure. We do not know if there are equivalents in the human psyche. If there are it does not seem that they are brought into play automatically as is true in the body. We are much clearer on the conditions that are necessary for body healing than we are where psychic healing is concerned. These have been arrived at through years of conscious, systematic exploration and testing. There was a time not long ago when a person was kept completely immobilized following surgery. Today individuals sit up and walk just hours after major surgery has been performed removing such organs as the gall bladder, the appendix, the reproductive system. A week in the hospital, six weeks of moderate activity and the body is as good as new, often with no aftereffect to the massive organ removal.

Where the psyche is concerned a very different situation seems to exist. Why after 10 years is the loss of a spouse recalled with such poignancy, the hurt as intense, as vivid as when it first happened? Why the panic, the disequilibrium, the affront to self-esteem, to internal and external security? Does the psyche have less self-healing capacity than the body? Or is it that we do not know yet the conditions necessary to promote psychological healing; to help the psyche develop mechanisms, skills to compensate for what has been lost? Is the psyche capable of complete restoration after a major onslaught to its equilibrium? It was in an effort to find answers to these questions that I undertook to be a guinea pig on the subject of loss when sudden death brought an end to my marriage of 43 years, an end to a relationship that had been central to my life for half a century. We had lived in our home for almost 25 years. I had never been there alone at night. We had had no children. I was alone in the most intrinsic sense: no parents, no siblings, no children. An extended family did exist, but no primary ties to provide anchorage or the pillars around which to weave my life. A network of friends, of course. But again no one on whom I had any claim; no one who owed me anything. A bleak, dismal reality. A void without boundaries. It helped to be reminded by those who cared that the future comes a day at a time, a moment at a time and should be dealt with accordingly. There were repeated assurances that "time heals." Now, 2¹/₂ years later, evidence is still lacking for me. The loss, the pain is as intense as it was when it first happened. Nothing I have done and I have done much—traveling across country for radio and TV appearances, newspaper interviews on my new womb-imprint theory, workshops, writing—nothing has touched the pain of the loss. A young cousin of mine widowed three years before put it accurately I believe: "It doesn't get better," said she. "One just learns to live with it." Perhaps 2½ years is not a long enough period to make a judgment where a relationship of half a century is concerned. But at this point in my experience I would concur. It doesn't get better. One somehow learns to live with it. Two questions surface and will be the focus of this presentation: Why doesn't it get better? How does one learn to live with it?

Why Doesn't It Get Better?

In the more than 40 years that I have been in clinical practice I have always alerted people that there was risk in an in-depth, committed relationship. That risk was the ever-present possibility of loss. For myself whenever I prayed it was for one thing: strength to deal with whatever life had in store. And it was the development of strength for dealing with life's eventualities that over the years was a treatment goal in my clinical practice. I have known the right words. I did not know what I was talking about. I had believed the researcher who many years ago concluded that the system responds to vicarious experience just as it does to the real experience. Maybe it is true in many situations. Where the loss of a spouse by death is concerned it is not true. No way could the ego survive repeated vicarious experiencing of the level of loss that is entailed in this specific situation. It is too devastating. At least it is too devastating as our psyches are presently constituted. Being the futurist and the evolutionist that I am, I hold out the hope that perhaps we can so constitute the psyche that the devastation is less total, less pervasive.

A dear friend of long-standing marveled along with me. We had survived the loss of parents. This had occurred in our adulthood. She had survived the loss of several siblings. All with reasonable equanimity. But the death of her husband after years of illness, and the death of mine in a matter of hours had shaken our psychic equilibrium. It didn't make sense. She and I had been career women. My marriage had been somewhat more concentrated perhaps because we had no children and our extended family was sparse. But we had both been autonomous, self-directing individuals. What was amiss in our psychic equipment? What had been lacking in our psychic development? Was there something more we could have done to have bolstered ourselves against the eventuality that strikes as many as 85% of the married women today, widowhood? What can we do, what must we do if we as individuals are to make the most of the time that remains for us to live?

One thing of which we were sure was that we would never forget what we had had. Equally clear was that we could not live on what had been and be alive. We could mark time until our own death. We knew many people who did just that. But for us that would be the equivalent of dying with death itself an aftermath. it was in January 1953 on the occasion of my mother's death that I wrote:

Aftermath

Death comes.
But not the moment
That the heart is numbed to rhythm
And the brain to hurt.

When wonder ceases
And each moment bears
But burden to a pain; and eyes
Seek naught but affirmation
Of a fruitless wish
There is no life.

When life has ceased
Death comes—an aftermath.

We were reeling but we did not want to surrender. What would it require to survive, perhaps even to master our new reality and somehow learn to make the most of it?

There is one incontrovertible fact: loss is. Equally incontrovertible is: endings and loss are synonomous. Some endings involve more loss than others. The extent of the loss is directly related to how central, how much of one's life the loss affects. Some losses can be replaced. Some losses can be circumvented, detoured. Some losses are mitigated with time. Some losses are forever and irreconcilable. They must be suffered like the chronic pain for which there is no cure; like the incurable illness. There may be palliatives that reduce or give temporary relief from the pain. There may be activities that distract, divert attention from the hurt.

The issue is psychic injury: To what extent has the psyche been traumatized? What resources does the psyche have to deal with the trauma? Are those resources adequate to full restoration of the psyche? Can there be full restitution or must the individual be content with repair, with adaptation? What would signify full restitution, restoration? What are the criteria we would use to indicate full psychic health?

A systematic search for psychic interventions comparable to those that have been developed for healing of the physical body is urgently needed. Psychic injury can be life threatening. Statistics on illness, death, suicide among those who have experienced the ending of a significant relationship whether by choice or by forces beyond human control confirm this beyond doubt. Psychic trauma can spread. It can affect the physical organism. It can generate or activate psychical conditions that place the physical organism in jeopardy, even destroy it. And of course the psyche can decide that the suffering is too great to endure. Ending by choice, surrender to nothingness wins over the continuing struggle to live.

I was shocked when one of my peers commiserating with me on my loss stated simply, firmly that if anything happened to her husband she would commit suicide. Here was a bright, accomplished senior of our society saying that life alone was more than she could bear. Her grown children and her growing grandchildren provided neither purpose nor solace enough for survival. Even greater shock gripped me as one of my younger friends, a beautiful woman in her early fifties with three accomplished children and proven abilities of her own in the business world, stated the very same thing in the very same words.

Perhaps I had not been as far off-track as I sounded when I announced to my friends that if I didn't "make it" I would come out publicly with all of my professional authority and declare that love was not good for the psyche. If love withdrawn leaves destruction, if the psyche having been privileged with love cannot survive without it, two questions surface: Is the psyche's need for love insatiable? Does love debilitate; does it stunt development of the equipment necessary for individuals to survive in a mobile, rapidly changing world?

These are important questions. They may signal issues crucial to human survival in a volatile world of ever-expanding dimensions.

I had been equally taken aback when a very dear friend finding it difficult to witness my distress commented that maybe it would have been better if my husband and I had died together. Of course. Death is no problem. Life is a problem. I would have been spared the unbearable.

I find no comfort in the common cliché: Everything happens for the best. I do not believe that. Some things are bad without qualifications. They have no redeeming features. One must make the best of what happens, and to the best of one's ability, consistent with one's view of self, of life and of community. That is the challenge for those who choose to fulfill the contract that comes with life, i.e., to live.

Other Realities

It was a shock. It was a shock for which I was not prepared. I had been on my seventh radio-TV tour in 10 months. I had been well received in New York, in Chicago by young talented talk show hosts and by sophisticated hosts of many years of experience. For good reason I had been on "cloud nine" and then whammo—HOME—and a depression the like of which I had never before experienced. It didn't make sense. But then neither did the panic, the physical discomfort that had marked my original reaction.

It was the panic, the physical distress that had led me into my exploration of the unconscious a year and a half before. It was the exploration into the unconscious that had led to my womb-imprint theory in February of 1978, three months after Gene's death. It was the womb-imprint theory that led me to the new findings in brain research. It was the new findings in brain research that took me into the study of brain anatomy and the neural network approach to psychotherapy.

Here I was 21 months after Gene's death experiencing life-threatening depression. True, it was holiday time. Loss combined with holiday is a lethal combination. Cloud nine had completely dissipated. At best it is illusive, nonsubstantive. On home territory it dissipates quickly. In fact it often lacks even its ephemeral existence. Questions: What is it all about? What good is it? What does it matter? To whom, if anybody does it matter? These flooded my psyche. Thank goodness for two young protegés who reminded me that I was doing what I was doing because I believed that what I had to say was important and I wanted to make it available to the general community. They were obviously distressed that I was bringing my goals into question. Seven tours, 70 programs in 11 months across country and without a book to sell: Wasn't that proof that what I was saying was well received? My logical mind concurred. What I was experiencing was not logical. Where was it coming from?

Loss and the Anatomy of the Brain

For the purposes of this discussion visualize the brain as diamond-shaped. Segment the lowest angle to include one-fifth of the organ. This is the limbic section, the oldest, often designated as the reptilian brain because its equivalent is found even today in reptiles. The limbic section houses the emotions: love, hate, anger, aggression. It is the locus of the autonomic system: breathing, appetite, circulation. Next in evolutionary seniority is the right hemisphere. It is approximately 2½ million years old (the limbic section is approximately 3 million years old). The right hemisphere is where the "gods" of primitive man resided. It houses the mandates and taboos of tradition and family and socialization procedures. It is the home of archaic fantasies that some hypothesize may come via the genes. The right hemisphere has both visual and auditory capacity (dreams). It can sing but not speak. It can write poetry but not rhyme. It is a master at spatial relationships and math. It is the source of imagination. Equal in size with the right hemisphere but much younger in evolutionary history is the left hemisphere. Archaeologists venture that the left hemisphere came into existence approximately 300,000 years ago when the brain doubled in size. The left hemisphere houses the capacity to speak. It cannot sing. The left hemisphere accumulates knowledge, has a keen sense of time and sequence and reality (to which the right hemisphere pays no attention). The left hemisphere is the source of judgment and reason.

Covering the top of the right and left hemispheres like a blanket is a narrow sheath of neural fibers.[6] This probably is the very youngest part of the brain. From the activity taking place here one may assume this is the locus of the ego. It is the part of the brain where the decisions are made as to which stimuli go where. In this neural sheath would be what Freud has called the guardian or the gatekeeper, the selecting-directing mechanism. In this area of the brain would be values, priorities, goals, the guidelines for stimuli distribution. It is possible that this area of the brain would be responsible for the "origin of consciousness" which Julian Jaynes dates to having taken place only about 3,000 years ago.[7]

Noam Chomsky, a researcher at MIT has ventured that the human mind is "a set of separate mental organs," each as "distinct and as faithful to its own rules of operation as the heart, liver and eye." The connecting link is the corpus callosum. Consisting of an incalculable number of neuron fibers, the corpus callosum keeps each section in touch with what is going on in the other sections.[8] It is when each section functions in harmony with the values, priorities, goals of the neuron sheath that the individual functions maximally.

As I considered my reactions within the framework of the above, I had to face up to certain questions. Was there some question in my mind—in the neural sheath of my brain as to whether I had a right to live life fruitfully? Was my decision to remain in the house we had shared for 25 years indication that I was enjoying my pain? (This had been suggested by one of my friends when I indicated that home was where I wanted least to be, though moving was unthinkable.) My logical mind was clear: I had a right to be; I had a right to live fully, productively. My right hemisphere was certainly functioning well for never had my mind been as searching, as creative. The problem then must be coming from my limbic system. The limbic system which one might well characterize as: I want what I want when I want it and for always. Researchers have alerted us to the fact that the neural connections between the limbic system and the left hemisphere are sparse. Perhaps mine were underdeveloped. Perhaps my limbic system had not been apprised of realities or perhaps in its characteristic self-centered way it was paying no attention to what my left hemisphere was saying.

Operating on these possibilities I decided to act consciously, deliberately, firmly so that there would be no question as to what were going to be the controlling factors in my life. I was brief. I made it clear: I would not move. I loved my home. I could manage it. Any change I would make now would reflect my loss and not the vibrancy of the life I have had.

Still speaking to the limbic section of my brain I acknowledged that a loss of something that had existed for 43 years might be something from which it could not recover. Perhaps it was like having chronic arthritis or an incurable illness. People lived under those conditions, perhaps not happily; but they lived. Happiness was not the issue. Perhaps we had had our share of happiness. The cocoon was gone. The being loved no-matter-what was gone. There was a new reality. How could we make the most of it? That was the question. That was the challenge.

Interestingly, I have been better. I am able to come home earlier. I am able to go home for dinner instead of to a restaurant—not often, but I can do it. Just the other day (February 24, 1980) I cooked for the first time. I have been on two radio and TV tours in New York since my confrontation with the limbic section and I have managed the return home with greater ease, with nowhere near the level of depression I experienced in September 1979. I have managed these returns differently however. I planned activities so that my return would not be marked by empty unscheduled time. Unscheduled time, like holidays, is anathema to the human psyche when one is struggling with the pain of loss.

How Does One Learn to Live With It?
Steps in Dealing With Loss

My confrontation with the limbic system of my brain was the most recent of the interventions I used to deal with my new reality. Whether it will be the last remains to be seen.

To begin at the beginning. There were two questions I asked myself when my new reality hit:

1. What portion of my life was affected by Gene's death? I did a quick calculation: We had spent an average of 75 hours per week together. These would be the empty unscheduled hours I would have to find some way of filling.

2. What could I do now that I would not have considered doing during my marriage? I would be free to take on professional responsibilities that involved traveling. Many years before I had decided that traveling would not be good for my marriage and turned down many professional opportunities that would have required my being away. Even as I considered my new option I recognized the possibility that my marriage may just have been an excuse. Maybe I didn't have the ability to be truly mobile. This I would have to see. Another question touching on this was: Would I be able to be professionally venturesome; or was I able to be venturesome only because I had roots in a committed relationship. I have known professional people whose creativeness and general adventuresomeness ended with the end of marriage. Would I fall into the category of those who can fly only within the confines of external boundaries? Would I be able to fly free without external boundaries, with only those boundaries which I chose to establish and that would be consistent with my values, priorities and goals? These questions could be answered only with time.

Concurrent and overlapping with these two broad questions of free time and flying free were three other issues which I categorized as the *Three M's for Dealing with Loss: Management, Mastery, Maximizing.*

MANAGEMENT

Management is the simplest of the three tasks. It deals with the realities, the technicalities of property, finances, delegation of responsibility and authority. What the surviving spouse is unable to deal with must be delegated so that the realities are responsibly dispatched.

MASTERY

Originally I had thought of mastery as the second step, a step preliminary to maximizing. Now, 2½ years later I realize that mastery of the loss is not essential to maximizing one's potential in one's new reality. In fact, I consider as a very real possibility, that loss may not be masterable. The injury to the limbic system may be so profound that whatever restorative processes exist may be inadequate to the psychological task. The psyche then is faced with dealing with a chronic injury or disability in whatever compensatory ways it has available. It is indeed very much in the position of the body when it must accommodate to an incurable condition or a chronic condition for which only palliative measures are available. The most significant finding stemming from my experience is that loss must not be mastered in order for maximizing to occur.

MAXIMIZING

Maximizing, when it stems from a situation involving loss of a person central to one's life has very distinctive characteristics. It is first of all not an "ego trip." It is instead a survival technique. It is the lifeline. People marvel at my energy, my mobility, my availability. They do not believe me when I share that I am barely surviving; that I am still struggling to "keep my head above water." The image I project is quite different from what I experience. Work, hard work, work involving questions quite beyond my knowledge and comprehension provide my only reprieve, my only solace. I am impressed with what my mind has been willing to tackle and what it has achieved. I do not understand its level of adventuresomeness or its level of creativity. I appreciate it. I nurture it. I enjoy it. And in "going public" as I have I am exploiting it but in what I consider a most responsible way.

A young talk show host was puzzled by what I was doing. He was very much aware of what it was costing to have an agent to arrange radio and TV appearances that yielded no income and with no prospect of any personal or financial gain. He opened the half-hour talk show with the question: "What do you want in your epitaph?" I was taken aback to be sure. It was such a straightforward question. Not hostile. Not disparaging. He was puzzled; sincerely puzzled. There were two words I would like in my epitaph: "She Cared." He accepted this without comment and the interview proceeded. At the end I wound up my remarks: "When the curtain goes down, I would like to feel that I had tried."

In one of my very first talk show appearances in New York (November 1978), the young talk show host asked me, again soberly, again respectfully: "Do you really think you can change the world all by yourself?" "Individuals have been known to make a difference," I answered, "and I would like to try." I have been on that program four times and have an open invitation to return whenever I am in the area. It is a station that reaches 600,000 young people, one of the few stations in the country with a young audience.

What I am doing makes no sense economically. The cost is phenomenal. It makes no sense egoistically. There is no glamour to the project. Mass media personnel barely say hello and only occasionally do they say "Thank you." You are a part of their job; a part of the passing scene. And there is no feedback. The stations receive reactions but they do not pass them on. So one works in a vacuum. What a tough task it is to have to pull oneself up by one's own psychological bootstraps over and over again; to have to convince oneself, over and over again that what one has set out to do is worth the money, time, effort, energy. How can one possibly know if it is. The only thing I know is that there is nothing I would rather do. And so in the interest of survival I an indulging myself; and along the way trying to make the very most out of every experience. There is no pot of gold at the end of the rainbow. If I do not make the most of the passing scene there is nothing. In the meantime my mind is having fun with its excursions and I an having fun with my mind.

Prerequisites to Maximizing

Maximizing does not just happen. There are certain preconditions, certain prerequisites. First there is the matter of bringing under control arational interferences from the two archaic sections of the brain: the limbic system and the right hemisphere. There are the practical issues of health, energy, finances, obligations. There are philosophical issues of rights, priorities, goals. Finally there is the course of action for picking up the pieces and charting the balance of one's life.

CONTROL OF ARATIONAL INTERFERENCES.

"What does one do when panic strikes," I asked one of the youngest people I know, 85 years young, a widow of 15 years. "Stop whatever you're doing and do something else," she said simply, firmly. It worked as I struggled with the compulsive rumination, the reliving of those last crucial hours when my world was in the balance and finally collapsed. How come it worked? How come it worked so effectively that even if I try it is virtually impossible to bring the compulsive rumination, the broken record into operation? It was this question that led me to new brain research and the findings that resulted in the development of my neural network approach to mental health intervention.

To use the neural network approach in dealing with arational interferences from the right hemisphere and the limbic system, there are three steps: (1) awareness—one must be aware of when the arational interferences occur; (2) one must stop them as soon as one becomes aware of them for they become quickly entrenched in their compulsive, round-robin pattern. To stop them one must bring into play the left hemisphere. The left hemisphere points out that what the archaic sections of the brain are doing is not logical, not necessary, not appropriate, and they are to stop. If they do not stop, if the compulsive rumination continues, (3) stop whatever you are doing and do something else. Two theories operate here. The mind can concentrate on only one thing at a time. In changing the point of concentration one cuts off the flow of energy coming from the inappropriate activity. Research on laboratory animals and on newborn infants suggests that if the neural network is not exercised it atrophies. New neural networks are established through use of new stimuli.[9]

Stopping the energy flow from compulsive rumination frees it for use on other mental activities. Often, stopping compulsive rumination improves sleep and adds to the general store of energy available for activities. If one is not able to use the three-step approach, one must examine one's commitment. Is one committed to living or to memorializing the dead? Is one committed to one's right to live, to live fully, according to one's highest potential? If there is any conflict, confusion, ambivalence one will not be able to use the neural network approach with sufficient consistency to stop the round-robin pattern of memory or to bring about the atrophying of that section of the neural network that is yielding arational interferences with reality performance.

Free of the preoccupation with the ending, one can begin to address oneself with the issues that pertain to a new beginning. "Every end is a beginning," said T. S. Eliot. "The end is where we start from."

PHILOSOPHICAL ISSUES.
A young friend having listened to an account of one of my tours queried: "Do you mean to say that you sold yourself short during your marriage?" "Of course," I replied. I had done it consciously, deliberately and fully consistent with my values, priorities and goals. What is more, I would do it all over again if there were the choice. For there was nothing in what I was doing that was comparable in any way to what my marriage had offered and provided. In no way did it compensate for what I had lost. That does not mean that I am interested in replacement. I am not. I plead with my very well-meaning friends not to consider me "eligible" or "available." Another in-depth relationship with the kind of commitment I would be inclined to make is not the way I want to use the time and energy left to me as I fulfill the contract of life.

Having had all that I have had and having done everything within my power in deference to it, I feel no obligation to my past. I have no fear that I will forget it. It is in the marrow of my bones; in every sinew of my being. My problem is to let what has been be and to move on from there.

Philosophers have observed that often in a crisis one must be courageous or perish. And there was Winston Churchill who ventured that courage generates other qualities. Hopefully, this is true.

Free of worry about disloyalty to one's past, convinced that one has the right, perhaps even the obligation to make the most of oneself—one's natural endowment plus what one has gleaned from one's life experience—one needs to address oneself to goals. What does one want the content of life to be? What knowledge, what skills are necessary to make this possible? What effort, what energy are necessary and are they available?

One had best take inventory of one's resources: economic, psychological, social. And then move on to considering how each of these can be brought into play most efficiently, effectively so that they yield the greatest psychological return. For it is the psyche that is in distress when one is dealing with the loss of a central figure in one's life. It is the psyche that must be given first claim to internal and external resources.

Each person must examine the conditions that provide maximum opportunity for mastery. Some people find memory lane consoling, comforting. Others including myself find memory lane devastating, a deterrent to mastery, to healing of psychic distress. Some people find crying cathartic. For me, crying is an abyss of boundless dimensions. To survive I must avoid memory lane and the people who see me only in terms of what has been. They drain my psychic resources. They leave me debilitated, mired in loss and pain. I avoid them. They pose a risk to my survival.

Having taken inventory, having assessed assets and liabilities, the sources of strength and risk, one is ready then to consider next steps: Where does one want to begin the journey into the future? Here memories serve as an emotional bank account upon which one can draw. One's past can give one clues on interests, aptitudes, preferences. Achievements are a reservoir of skills, knowledge. They can provide guideposts in charting the new course. They can provide the wherewithal for decision-making; for the determination of goals. The deferred dream, the frustrated venture, or the challenge of the emerging world can provide the necessary impetus, the springboard to the future.

Two realities converge and place maximization in jeopardy.

They are two stark realities, incontrovertible and constant. To maximize one's potential requires hard work, hard work—without end. And there is no cocoon to come home to, no place where one is assured love, appreciation, no-matter-what; where one is shielded from the indifferences of the world.

It happened at a busstop in Florida. We struck up an acquaintance. The young lady was on her way to the U.N. for a field placement in international relations. She was working on her master's at MIT. I had just come from the I-CAPP Conference in Charleston, South Carolina. My comments about my womb-imprint theory opened the door. She told me she had lived with a young man for three years. They had broken up. She had worried that she would never fall in love again. But she did. She found however that love came packaged with dependency and that she did not want. Part of her warned that she should marry and have children so that she would belong. Her parents had been married 35 years. They didn't have to talk to each other. They knew intuitively how each felt and responded accordingly. I told her how I was missing most of all the cocoon that my marriage had provided.

Her face clouded as she soberly, empathically responded: "The cocoon has to be in yourself." What a lot of wisdom for a 24-year-old. I asked her how she was managing that. She went jogging every morning. She loved to write. She spent her free time at the typewriter.

Is it possible to build an internal cocoon? I don't know. At this moment I feel more as though what I am building is a new hub for my wheel, a new center of gravity. To find oneself alone for the first time in one's life; to find oneself without the person who for 50 years had been central to one's every thought, wish, plan is overwhelming.

"Author, Author, New Script, Please"

It is a shock to find oneself center stage, alone. No one in the wings. No coach. No prompter. No critic. No observer. And most distressing of all no prepared script and no author to prepare one. Writer, actor, producer, audience all rolled up into one—oneself. It is frightening. It can be immobilizing. It can be life threatening. When nothing seems to make sense, when the effort and energy required just to exist seems prohibitive, one must check out first of all the level of one's physical energy. Tiredness when it combines with futility is risky. One must be careful not to undertake more than one can manage. The 4-year-old, when his mother asked him why he always fell when he ran, answered confidently, "Because I always run faster than I can." There was no doubt in his mind that one day he would be able to run without falling. Somewhere on the road to adulthood we seem to have lost that confidence: the confidence that if we can't do it today, that doesn't mean we won't be able to do it tomorrow. We need to rediscover or redevelop that confidence. For the human being continues to be in a state of evolution just as is the world in which we live.

The fact that people in general today have difficulty dealing with loss when that loss involves someone central to life does not mean that this will always be true. Perhaps we will find ways of equipping the psyche so that it can have the pleasure of a long-term, in-depth, committed relationship without risking survival when the relationship ends. In the meantime, we are where we are and must deal with the situation accordingly.

First of all there is the new script. Conscious, deliberate decisions are necessary in its preparation.

- Do you want to mark time or make time count?
- Do you want to live the balance of your life in a rocking chair or in a trial balloon?
- Do you want the backyard to be your world, or your world to be your backyard?
- Do you want to settle for your roots, or do you want your roots to be the launching pad for your wings?

Perhaps before you can know for sure how you want your script to read you will need to explore, experiment.

- Investigate the options available to you, internal, external.
- Venture something new, something different, preferably some-

thing that has adventure in it. Do this even if you are unsure, afraid. Remember that success builds on success and tends to generalize. By the same token, insecurity and fear can generalize and immobilize.

- Avoid memory lane—the situations that remind you of what you have lost; and that what you have had will never be again.
- Don't permit your mind to meander down the road of the "might-have-beens" and the "should-have-dones." The past is irretrievable. One must forgive oneself for being human and indulge oneself in the privilege of being alive. Commitment to life and living is the only viable lifeline.
- Be as pretty as you can be. And finally,
- Splurge—be nice to you. Do for yourself what gives you a good feeling, what enhances your self-esteem.

The body for healing needs rest and nurturing. The psyche for healing needs distraction, diversion, and challenge. For it to achieve health and maximum functioning the psyche needs to have a sense of future not in terms of goals but in terms of experiencing; experiencing the untried, the unknown. It needs a sense of continuity: how its past can enrich and enliven its future. Our minds need to be fed and practiced to develop our imagination, our curiosity, our resourcefulness, our initiative, our courage. Life, unlike money, cannot be hoarded. It dissipates whether it is experienced or not. Therefore life should be spent to the very fullest of the resources with which we are endowed.

Notes

1. Wolman, Benjamin B., ed., *International Encyclopedia of Psychiatry, Psychology and Neurology*, vol. 10 (New York: Van Nostrand Reinhold, 1977), pp. 401–430.

2. Pines, Maya, *The Brain Changers* (New York: Harcourt Brace Jovanovich, 1973).

3. Wolman, op. cit., pp. 429–430.

4. Asimov, Isaac, *The Human Brain* (Boston: Houghton Mifflin, 1964), p. 3.

5. Pelletier, Kenneth R., *Toward a Science of Consciousness* (New York: Dell, 1978), p. 259.

6. Rayner, Claire, ed., *Body and Mind* (New York: Rand McNally, 1978), pp. 116–121.

7. Jaynes, Julian, *The Origin of Consciousness and the Breakdown of the Bicameral Mind* (Boston: Houghton Mifflin, 1976), pp. 307–313, 325.

8. Gardner, Howard, "Strange Loops of the Mind," *Psychology Today* (March 1980), pp. 78–79.

9. Wolman, op. cit., pp. 401–430.